TRANSITIONS

TRANSITIONS

A SPIRITUAL EVOLUTION

RICHARD D. RIDDLE SR.

iUniverse, Inc.
Bloomington

Transitions
A Spiritual Evolution

Copyright © 2011 by Richard D. Riddle Sr.

All rights reserved. No part of this book may be used or reproduced by any means, graphic, electronic, or mechanical, including photocopying, recording, taping or by any information storage retrieval system without the written permission of the publisher except in the case of brief quotations embodied in critical articles and reviews.

The views expressed in this work are solely those of the author and do not necessarily reflect the views of the publisher, and the publisher hereby disclaims any responsibility for them.

iUniverse books may be ordered through booksellers or by contacting:

iUniverse
1663 Liberty Drive
Bloomington, IN 47403
www.iuniverse.com
1-800-Authors (1-800-288-4677)

Because of the dynamic nature of the Internet, any web addresses or links contained in this book may have changed since publication and may no longer be valid. The views expressed in this work are solely those of the author and do not necessarily reflect the views of the publisher, and the publisher hereby disclaims any responsibility for them.

Any people depicted in stock imagery provided by Thinkstock are models, and such images are being used for illustrative purposes only.
Certain stock imagery © Thinkstock.

ISBN: 978-1-4620-1738-6 (sc)
ISBN: 978-1-4620-1737-9 (dj)
ISBN: 978-1-4620-1736-2 (ebk)

Library of Congress Control Number: 2011906651

Printed in the United States of America

iUniverse rev. date: 05/09/2011

NATHANIEL

RICHARD D. RIDDLE SR.

DEDICATION

I would like to dedicate this book to my family. They stood beside me through the many transitions of my life. Some have given more than can be imagined. It is through my love for each of them that I am able to focus my energy and continue my evolutionary journey.

I would also like to express my deepest appreciation and love for the dear and special friends in my life. Of these, I especially recognize Cyd, my spiritual advisor, friend, and counsel. Through the challenges of my evolutionary journey, she has stood next to me, giving me strength and encouragement.

On the spiritual side, I gratefully acknowledge, and thank from the deepest depth of my inner self, all those who stand over, protect, and guide me forward, while not interfering with my freedom of choice. To all of my friends and protectors, I cannot begin to list all your names. Knowing you are there gives me great comfort. Your existence is the proof of this writing. The gifts you have given are immeasurable, your love infinite.

I need to thank him, humiliated and tortured, hanging there on the cross, looking down on all of his tormentors, struggling even in those last moments to send the message of God's love. Yet *thank you* is just a phrase; it has no meaning without action. May I find the right action to convey my true love and appreciation.

Above everyone else, I thank God for the gift of life that I might enjoy all things.

In loving memory:

Of all those that have touched my life and passed on, returning home, I thank them all for their contribution to my plan and offer my congratulations to them for the completion of theirs. The latest of those passing on was my faithful and loving companion, Bailey, who shared my morning walks and offered her unconditional love each and every day. Bailey was my eight-year-old blood hound; I shall miss her.

TRANSITIONS

He: "Know that God loves you, so simple, but so difficult to comprehend by so many. How could something so simple be so hard to see? But it is the nature of man, to make it difficult to understand."

CONTENTS

About the Cover

In the week before Thanksgiving 2009, my son sat in the kitchen, visiting with his mother and me. It was late in the evening, and I offered him a small drink, a small measure of scotch. He relaxed, smiled, thought of smoking a cigar, and then asked for a sheet of paper and pen. When I returned with the items that he had requested, I noticed that he was "in spirit." What happened next was more moving than I can describe. His hand, holding the pen, swiftly and effortlessly moved across the paper, leaving lines here and there.[1] When he took his arm away, he presented me with the symbol seen on the cover of this book.

One could find a specific meaning for this symbol, or each of the symbols that make up the whole, with full detail, origin, and history. One could visually interpret the symbol, finding artistic imagery in the various shapes and curvatures. One could even emotionally interpret the symbol by looking closely and finding what feelings or emotions it invokes, perhaps a combination thereof or a combination of all three, for that matter.

Much like the symbol on the cover, the stories included within this book have many parts, their true meaning always there, just needing to be uncovered. These include the stories of my youth and discussions with my spiritual advisor, with my son, and with angels. Each of these experiences can stand alone as information on a sheet of paper, a recording, a phone conversation, or a memory; however, when

---

[1]   I do not say that he drew a symbol, it was more like uncovering a symbol that already existed on the paper.

1

combined together, they form something far more elaborate: a spiritual journey.

I do not expect that everyone that reads this book will truly comprehend The information or agree with it. Whether you do, or don't, the choice is left up to you. Freedom of choice is a gift from God; it is not my place to question, judge, or manipulate your thoughts. This book is a recollection of thoughts, messages, and communications. My hope is that something worthwhile within these pages will touch the heart of just one of you. Please do not overthink the information as provided. Among the messages is the single and most important message of all: "God loves you, each and every one, equally and with infinity!"

I ask you to open your heart, mind, and ears. Hear them and the message that they give to you. Know that we are not alone; sit back, relax, and take a spiritual journey with me.

PREFACE

I started to write an instructional book about spirituality. Upon further thought, I decided that doing so would be an exercise in futility, as spirituality is not physical and therefore is not constrained by our universe. Instead, I have chosen to write an autobiography, recounting the details of my life that have contributed to my own ongoing and eternal spiritual transitions.

The idea of spirituality can be described much like a mathematical singularity. A singularity is a zero-dimensional object that has no width, height, or depth; it is a point and easily exists in the mind or in theory. The difficulty is in proving its existence. A singularity can be described in great detail by mathematicians, but the moment that someone tries to represent it or depict it, then it ceases to be what it is defined to be. Even if you were to draw the smallest point possible on a piece of paper, through some form of measurement the height, width, and depth can be ascertained. It has become a three-dimensional object; it no longer is zero-dimensional. This is the problem that I have with writing about spirituality. I cannot represent correctly on paper that which cannot be defined. The only thing I can do correctly is tell you the story of what I have witnessed and done.

I am writing *Transitions* to tell you about my spiritual evolution. To do this I, first, introduce my motivation and then provide some background information. The autobiographical sequence of my life coincides with the linear journey of my spiritual evolution. I present different transitional points, first showing how my social personality was formed and then showing the subtle responses to my pleas for God's help; these responses were invisible to me then but are better understood now.

The next sections of *Transitions* show the parallelisms that exist in my life. In these sections, I often repeat a discussion given earlier in order to show how the same information can be perceived differently. What this means is that when I look back at what occurred, I can often find the positive and negative aspects of each event. Then I work to unfold those events to show that the negative events are often a part of the plan and may even be essential to the higher level plan that gives us freedom of choice.

For me, something happened that created a desire to learn more, to discover something spiritually that I had not known. This discovery has led me down a path that has permitted many changes in my life. I discuss things as simple as listening to the birds singing at sunrise to as complex as breaking an addiction to gambling and gluttony. These things that I have done are presented to provide an understanding of what can be done when there exists a desire to do something. *"Transitions occur, but they only occur if you want them to."*

Within *Transitions,* there will be text that is indented and italicized. I have done this to isolate actual spiritual discussions. I will show their words in the dialog with the preface "He:" and then present the text for what I received. I then preface text with "Me:" for my responses.

I have observed what I call three separate states of my son's physical and spiritual situation. In all of the states, Rich has left his body, or is "in spirit"; in some cases, another has taken possession. The exchange is witnessed from both the exit/incoming and the exit/returning conditions. The first part is somewhat subtle, the last a heartbreakingly painful experience to observe.[2] State one seems to be him, but not in the physical sense. In this state, he will present information and often refer

---

2   One, who said I could call him Leroy, explained to me that the pain of moving back from the "in spirit" state was intense. It could be compared to being hit by a truck, the latter being far less painful.

back to his human form. In this form, I have asked him what I should call him, and his response was, "Call me son." For state two, there is another that has exchanged positions with him. In this state, there is a direct dialog that takes place with one of many who have a message to deliver. It is in this state that I have had some of my most intense discussions with them. Finally, there is state three. In state three, he is outside his body and is describing what he sees and feels as he crosses into the "spiritual universe," if you allow me to use universe to explain a location that I cannot know or understand. It is in this state that he often described the physical feeling he experienced, or what he saw or heard. It is in this state that he also described the physical feelings as he passed from the physical world to the spiritual universe. Examples were the feelings of ice cold water running down his back, the beauty of the "blue," serenity, and the many that surround him. In a few cases, he has taken me on a journey of my past lives, to include a time when my current spirit guide, Don, and I walked as brothers. Don was my young brother, and we had gone fishing together. A tragic accident occurred that day on the water. The scene showed both of us on the shore with many people around us; they were only able to save me from dying that day. Don is here with me, he watches over and assists me each and every moment.

When reading these communications, read the context of the introduction to the communication and then the words to help identify to whom I am speaking. Similar to what you may read of Edgar Cayce, when returning back from being "in spirit," Rich never has any recollection of what was said or done. He often will feel frustrated about the time away, as it is a blank hole in his memory. As he recovers, he will often ask a single question: "Was it worth it?"

Next, I use terms like "He that came before" or "Him" to refer to someone that you might try to identify as Jesus from biblical reference. In most cases, this should be clear enough of my intent by the content under discussion, and it may be asked why I do not just call him by his biblical name. The reason that I do it this way is not to obscure or hide his identity, but because that is the way they refer to him. It is similar to why they refer to the Christian Bible as the Book of Robes.

For the collective group, I use "they" to mean all those that surround us and help us through our lives to include angels, spirits, and spirit guides.

I include notes that I collected during many visits to the home of Rich and his wife, Sumer. He would hand me his notes, from which I extracted many paragraphs to present here or used to assist my further understanding of what he is experiencing. This understanding has helped me on my own spiritual journey. Where used, each of these sections will also appear in italics. It is for this reason I have added his name as contributing author for *Transitions*. In all cases, I have tried to present these sections exactly as I read them so that you could feel what I felt at that first moment when they were presented.

Finally, I have spent hours upon hours with Rich, in person or on the phone, as he went through a very intense training period with them. Many of these conversations were difficult and intense. Mimi would often ask me what I was doing, why was all of this change necessary. I tried to explain to her, "I am here at this moment because he is here; I will be with him, no matter where he goes." Interestingly enough, it has never really been him that has needed the help, it has been me.

I have tried to present the information he has told me as accurately as possible. Sometimes it was not clear to whom I was speaking, and I would seek clarity. Sometimes I would get a name, sometimes not. One asked why I needed a name. He explained that names are superficial; do I just need a confirmation, something to research on the Internet? He said if I must have a name, then I could call him 1-1-3. I retaliated that I did not always do that. He challenged me on that statement, and I had to admit that he had me cold, as I had performed a search on most names and even searched the number to see if it was a documented angelic sequence.

I think a lot about all that has been revealed to me. I cannot include it all in *Transitions* but have included as much as I can to help you see what I have experienced.

I ask a simple question: "Why would they be there then and not be here today?" It doesn't make sense to me. I must be missing something. I listen intently; I try to assemble all of the pieces. From all of this, I derive the one most conclusive and singular constant and most significant revelation:

God loves you; they love you, so simple, so simple.

INTRODUCTION

They are all around us. They are here and have always been here. They will be here for eternity. Who are they? They are God, angels, spirits, positive energies, and negative energies. At first I lacked the confirmation of their existence, but today I feel their presence all around me. I witness the proof of their existence in all that I see, feel, and hear. It is for this reason that I write *Transitions*, to let you know what has occurred in my life that gives me this certainty. I want to share my experiences with you.

Transitions presents information that I have collected over the years. It summarizes my experiences, thoughts, and communications. What I have to say is not intended to attack or criticize you or what you are doing. It is not intended to discredit your religion or your beliefs. It is simply a summary of experiences I have had, things I have learned, and communications that I have received. I try to show you that God continues to send his messengers to deliver the common message to each and every one; he loves us, and the gift of love is the greatest gift of all. Despite this unconditional message, we as people continue to misinterpret the message, but that misinterpretation may be a part of the plan, a plan that provides complete freedom of choice.

As you read *Transitions,* you will undoubtedly encounter information that is foreign to your way of thinking. Some ideas may not be acceptable to you or may be in conflict with what you believe. I understand that this will occur. The explanation is simple: we as humans do not possess all knowledge, and that means that there is new and unfamiliar experiences and information that must be learned.

You have chosen to read *Transitions* and are therefore open to this new information. It is up to me to present you with something credible. My problem is that I cannot prove a single line presented herein. There is simply no known scientific representation or explanation. I have experienced things I know as truth, I have seen things that I thought I would never see, and I have heard words that I never thought I would hear spoken. After many years, culminated by more than two years of positive energy exercises and interactions, I have attempted to document the information that I have received so that I may share that information with you. I can only hope that I have recounted this information without misinterpretation.

I know that there is that which is said and that which is understood. I am challenged to represent the facts of what was said, not the facts of what was understood. An example of this is when you say to me, "This," but I understand you to say, "That." I then present to others my understanding that what you said was "That," rather than the truth that you really said "This." What I am really saying is that I think I know what I understood to be said, but I could be wrong, so read this with an open mind.

I try to understand the spiritual world and where I fit within that world. Through the journey I have learned the most important truth that we all need to know and understand. God loves us! Simple and pure, God is love, and God loves all of his children. Though this fact is simple, it is complex to understand the meaning. Its meaning is more powerful than the love of family; it is stronger than the force of gravity that holds us to the earth. It is, and always has been. It is eternity. God loves each and every one of us, equally, with infinity. He does not choose to love one more than another, he loves everyone the same. There are no exceptions, no privileges; you cannot earn favor in God's eyes, nor earn disfavor. God loves you, purely and completely. You do not need to beg for his forgiveness, his love is unconditional! This is what I have discovered. You may have known this already. You may say that everyone knows of God's love. Yet, there can be difficulty understanding the meaning of unconditional love.

Each and every day, someone puts a condition on love. I look at this thought closely and try to understand why it would be necessary to place something trite and superficial between myself and those I love. True love has no conditions. I write these words, my heart is bursting, filled with emotion; tears are streaming down my cheeks; I struggle to convey this emotion, the emotion of love. I will talk more about this later; for now, I am looking deeply into my own feelings, to understand love and to find a way to pass that understanding on to others. As I proceed with my own transition, perhaps I will be able to show you something new, perhaps not; my goal is to share with you my understanding of the facts presented to me.

Consider "facts" for a moment. A fact could be called a truth, and if a truth exists, then it is a truth because it exists, not because we agree it exists. If I look back into my history lessons, I recall the discussion of Christopher Columbus arguing that the world is round, contrary to the popular thought that the world appeared to be flat. The fact is the world is round, and therefore truth exists, but it was contrary to the popular belief of the time. The truth about the world did not change, only the belief changed when the truth was finally proven.

Consider another example. If I were to point into the universe and tell you a star was born over there, you could say that because you cannot see it, it was not born. If I were to tell you that it was so far away that its light will not reach the earth for a billion years or more, it would not change your belief that it was not born, nor my ability to prove that it occurred. If the star was born, then your ability to see it, or not see it, does not alter the truth of its birth. That truth exists does not change because of individual or group perceptions or understanding. Facts and truth are not controlled by popular thought or democratic vote, they just are. In the words of Gandhi, "An error does not become truth by multiplied propagation, nor does truth become error simply because no one sees it."

Finding truth for me is to understand that I do not possess it and therefore must seek new information that will get me closer to it. To get closer to the truth, I struggle to open my ears to hear what is said, to open my eyes to see what is presented, and to open my mind to understand it. Today I am only able to continue the search, and the more I discover, the more I find I need to learn. While later I will discuss the concepts of possessing knowledge versus seeking knowledge, for now I think that it is also important to say that it is not possible to completely understand and know everything. To suggest otherwise does not make sense. Similarly, as introduced earlier, I can provide what I understand, but that in all cases it will not be what was meant, when I wrote down what was said. It is not because I have not been diligent in capturing my notes and presenting them here. It is because of that which I will discuss later, a process called learning by reference. What this means is that we, in the general case, interpret what we hear in accordance with our reference database, or knowledge reference, meaning from what we already know.

FAVORS

Often, over the years, I have asked God for favors, for blessings of material goods, money, and success. I have often felt left out, abandoned, and ignored. No matter how hard I tried, it always seemed like I, or he, fell short in achieving my expectations. For all of the achievements that I have enjoyed, they never seemed enough; there was always the need for more. I needed more property, more money, more attention, more education, more everything. I would explain to God that if he were to give me a lot of money, I would use it for the good of all. With money, I could help family and friends. I could only imagine all that I could do, and I would dream of how to spend a million dollars. As I would dream, I would find that one million would not be enough; it must be ten million, then twenty million. It did not matter; I wanted a computer, then it must be faster; a house, and then it must be bigger.

I considered my request for a while and then was reminded of this simple, yet powerful message: "We ask God to give us all things so that we may enjoy life, but instead God gave us life so that we could enjoy all things." I sat and pondered this message. Not its general meaning, but instead its true meaning to me. I ask the question, "How do I fit into this message? How do I accept what God has given me and enjoy life?"

UNDERSTANDING

I seek understanding from God. I desire the understanding that the experience of life, its beauty, is the same, every day. I try to understand, without conditions, that it doesn't matter if it is cloudy or clear, the sun is shining or raining; every day is glorious. Each day is surrounded by God's love. Each day is beautiful, each and every one, all the time. When I am able to completely understand this, without restrictions, then I hopefully will achieve the next level of understanding, the next step forward in my spiritual evolution.

God loves you. His love is the most significant and complete fact that I have been told, read, heard, and that I now understand. His love is not dictated by a religion. Favoritism is not granted because of religious practice or heritage. The indications of receipt of his love are not shown by social status, position, wealth, or looks. His love is not restricted to race, gender, or personal preferences. His love is given to all, completely and without conditions. If I understand that single fact and then use it to better understand myself and others, then I may learn to love myself and, with that love of self, learn to share that love with others. We are created in the same essence of God, all of us. No one person was created different, given more, or given less, his essence is in all of us. All are created the same and share the same level of God's love. The depth of that love is eternal; it is infinite; if we choose to look for it, we can find it.

If given the opportunity to ask one and only one question and know that the answer would be given, then what question would I ask? What question is worthy of a universal answer? Should I ask how long I will live, what will happen tomorrow? Such questions seem so superficial, so what should I ask?

>He: *"You may ask two questions."*

>*My mind raced, I struggled to find the right question.*

>Me: *"There are so many questions, help me choose."*

>He: *"Choose two."*

I ultimately asked two questions, but after that I struggled with the questions that I asked and what I should have asked.

I asked coworkers what question they would ask, and in a later discussion with him, I told him what they said and my response. One said they would ask, "When will I die?" I said, "If you knew, what would you do different?" The response back was that if she knew that, she would go home and gather her family around her and let them know how much she loved them. I countered that since she did not know the answer and that any day could be the end, then why would she not do that each and every day? Later, during a morning walk, I engaged in a conversation with him and I recounted this discussion. His response was that the question was superficial and that the more accurate response to her question was that she was already dead. If she was waiting for the answer on when she would die to start living, then by not living she was, in essence, dead. He then stated that the better question to ask is, *"How do I love more?"* I continued walking, thinking on this, and then asked, "How do I love more?" His answer was, *"Learn to love yourself, who and what you are. You are made from the essence of God, the same as each and every other person; learn to love yourself, and then you will be able to love others."*

On a more global level, I think that the conflicts of politics, countries, and religions may be reduced to a single element. That element is the lack of love. Hopefully as you read this, you will begin to understand the depth of the love of God, the depth of your own love, and ultimately what you may do with it. It is upon this path that I choose to proceed. A path that is not straight or narrow, but meandering, wide, and strewn with obstacles. A thousand questions fill my mind, and amongst these questions are answers, yet the questions and answers are not paired; the pairing must be done by me.

ENERGIES

I will also try to address my understanding of negative energies. It will be complex to talk about these energies, as they do not like the idea of being uncovered for what they are. These energies would rather hide and deceive. When I understand and recognize their existence, and when I understand and practice God's love within myself, then I can discover that their power over me diminishes, but it does not disappear. If, on the other hand, I let the negative energies influence my actions, then I will only support the growth of their power.

You could say that you do not believe in negative energies, but please understand, they believe in you. When negative energies seek to influence your decisions or actions, they do not question your beliefs or limit their actions because you do not believe in them. Realize, they achieve their best results when you don't know they are there. It is also important to understand that their work is masked in your understanding of what is occurring. For example, an act that is the result of pride could be justified by saying the act was done to assist others. I might say that I argued for a political policy that, if promoted, could help thousands but take from a thousand others. Such a conflict would appear on both sides to be fought for others, not self. If we look at the argument closely, we can find that it is clouded in greed and pride from all involved and that the conflict it produces only increases the power of the negative forces that promoted the debate from its beginning.

Of comfort is the fact that regardless of your belief in God or his messengers, he and they also believe in you. They are always there to guide us and assist us, if only we ask. That does not mean that we are given everything that we ask for, because everything we really need is already here. All we need is God's love; we just need to open our ears, eyes, minds, and hearts to receive it.

SPIRITUALITY

If I say that I am spiritual, you may interpret this as a shortcut to a condition where I believe in God but use this word as an excuse or justification for not taking the time to go to a church or synagogue, or participate in religious activities. Yet, I often think that the term "spiritual" has taken on a different meaning for many people, perhaps more my own previous thought than others, with the perception being more negative than otherwise. Today I try to elaborate on the true meaning of spirituality and then in order to explain it better, I seek some physical representation of spirituality in the form of a single person. I think about it, and it could be that the most representational person would be the Dalai Lama (though he may not feel that way). I can see him as spiritual from my perspective. If I look at myself, it is clear that I can only see myself at the infant stage of any level of spiritual development. This is because spirituality is not about the word, it is about the action in support of the word.

I tried to find other examples, and by happenstance I watched an episode of Andrew Zimmern's *Bizarre World*, where he was with the Ju'hoansi people of the Kalahari Desert in Africa.[3] In this episode the tribe's shaman demonstrated their ability to communicate with the spirits by entering a spiritual state or trance. What occurred during those last minutes of the filming was very interesting. I observed a definite view of spirituality from my interpretation, but depending on their goal and the message they were communicating, it could be otherwise. As it continued, during one point in the episode, a shaman placed his hands on Andrew's diaphragm and back. The touch provoked an emotional response from Andrew that he admittedly could not explain. Later, the shaman spoke of God's love and the love that is inside of us, and when Andrew asked what he was to do with this, the shaman responded, "Share it with others." This summary of the event and its meaning was truly my understanding of spirituality.

So what are my thoughts or my interpretation of being spiritual? For me, spirituality is about God. I believe in God, I believe in God's love, and I believe that God provides us with his messengers to assist us in our daily lives. On the other hand, to contrast spirituality with religion, then for me, religion is about churches, synagogues, temples, shrines, and books. In my conversations with religious people, they always go to the book and tell me that the book says this or that. They read a single verse or a small section of a chapter and then go to a great deal of effort interpreting what they have read. They will talk about the years of sermons they have given or heard and mention what church

---

3   Permission granted by Mr. Zimmern.

or synagogue they attended. In a debate I observed between a person that does not believe in God and one that does, I found an interesting paradox. Both established the rule for the existence of God within the context of the book. One did not believe in the sanctity of the book, and therefore because the book said God exists and he did not believe in the book, he concluded God does not exist. The other argued for the sanctity of the book and believed that all within the book is accurate and God inspired. Therefore, the book exists, it is accurate, and thus God exists.

I could find little benefit to gain from either interpretation. To put God into a container, to limit his existence to such trite argument and justification, does not make sense. I have read the Bible from cover to cover; I have had courses in religion in college as a part of the core curriculum for my bachelor's degree. I have always believed that the books of religion were written by man, for man, and organized by man to control man. What I have learned is that those books were written by man, for man, and that there are sections and authors whose words could have been inspired by God. The books clearly have information that is historical in nature, but that information is interweaved with fictional stories, fables, parables, and metaphors, or even excerpts or plays, examples being the Song of Songs, a play excerpt, and the story of Job, a fable. I am not convinced that everything written in the books occurred the way the stories are told or interpreted, but it does not matter, as the stories are told in a convincing fashion, and many people benefit from those stories. Despite that benefit, I am not convinced that God directed their writing any more than he directs my writing of this book. That said, I am convinced that each author was supported by God during their writing of their books, and in some cases they may have been inspired by information they received, just as I receive assistance with the writing of this book, by my own request to them. The choice to write their books was their choice, just as the writing of this book is mine, and the choice of reading their books or this book is yours. As you continue reading this book, I ask that you not call out any chapter or paragraph as a quote of truth or lack of truth, but instead consider the totality of the information presented, and then seek your own truth, from all information presented to you.

To be complete, I should also add that much good has come from what is written in the various religious books. Most religious cultures practice love and compassion, therefore it is not appropriate that I criticize the words, what is understood in the words, or what is practiced as an interpretation of the words. I also believe that a lot of bad appears to have occurred as a direct result of the interpretation of what is written and practiced in those same religious cultures. The bottom line is that the universe operates on a harmonic rhythm, and with all things, there are ups and downs. How we react to these harmonic and often cyclic events makes all the difference in our lives. As I was raised in a Christian culture, my discussions later in the section "In God's Service" will be more directed toward information contained in the Bible, but they could also apply to other cultures. I believe that we the people, all people, are capable of being much more than what we show on the surface. We just need to understand how we fit within the universe. I will try to discuss that as well.

TRANSITIONS

On February 5, 2009, I was traveling on business, driving on Interstate 605, heading to the Los Angeles International Airport. My son called me and told me that his nightmares had returned, and they were worse than ever before. "They" tortured him, it was unbearable. This was not the first time we had spoke about the dreams and the torture. I had begged him before to let me take this burden from him; he had only looked at me with pain deep in his eyes and replied, "I would not give you this even if I could, I love you too much." On this day, driving down the road, I reminded him of God's love. I told him he must keep his thoughts on God and pray for God's love to protect him. We talked for almost an hour, then he said he was going to cook dinner for his wife. I told him how much I loved him, and then he hung up the phone.

Transitions for me are pivotal points in my life where I have moved from one path to another. It is like walking down a hallway and seeing a couple of doors. At this point, I made a choice to continue down the hall or enter a door on the right, or a door on the left. Any decision is the right decision in God's eyes, for he loves us no matter what choice we make. I understand that the conflict I experience daily, the decisions that I struggle to make, are my conflicts alone, and my decisions alone, and that they may often lead to a transition point in my life. As my life does not occur in solitude, I often find that my family will often try to assist me in my choices. They have the right to present their views and encourage me, and I respect that right. It is still my decision which path to take, as their input is just another door to consider, albeit an important door. I understand that others also have their own path to follow. They must make decisions that are right for them, it is their right to do so.

To help you understand me better, in terms of transitions, for over twenty years I have held the belief that anything can happen at any time and that the choices made at the moment can make all the difference.

An example of this is occurred in 1981; while going for an evening run in Lawton, Oklahoma, my son, who was six at the time, rode his bicycle alongside me. We approached an intersection. We were proceeding down the left side of the highway, facing oncoming traffic. My son was to my left; we approached a light-controlled intersection. At the same time, a pickup sped up to the light, the driver looking at traffic to his left, ignoring the right, as it was a divided highway and no traffic would be coming from that direction, or so he must have thought. Without stopping, he turned into us. As all of this unfolded, I realized that I had to somehow stop my son from being hit by the truck. To get the attention of the driver in hopes of stopping the truck in time, I raised by hands over my head, and then as the truck hit me full force, I brought my fist down on the hood. The driver immediately slammed on his brakes as the truck struck me and knocked me backward. My son's bicycle, being farther to the left, grazed the front tire of the truck, and then he and it came to a stop just in front of the rear tire.

I sat up on the shoulder of the roadway where I had landed, the driver rushing to my side. He was obviously terrified by what had just occurred. Anxiously he asked if I needed an ambulance or whether he should take me to the hospital. My son Richie had just picked himself up from where he and his bicycle landed and ran to my side. He looked at the man and said, "My dad don't need to go to any hospital, he needs to finish his run." I looked at him and then the man and said, "Yes, he is right, I am fine, I need to finish my run." With that, I picked myself up from the roadway, Richie retrieved his bicycle, and we resumed our run.

It was only last year that Rich spoke of a situation where someone was given the choice to see the future and, from that vision, allowed to alter the outcome. It was a complex story about love and the choices we make. In the story, a woman saw a vision of her daughter being killed in a car accident. As she ran up the sidewalk toward her home, her teenage daughter was pulling away from the house, driving at residential speed toward her mother, who was frantically waving and screaming from the sidewalk for her daughter to stop. If she did not stop, she would get in an accident and her life would end. When I heard the situation, I could not guess what the mother could possibly do to prevent the family tragedy that was unfolding. He told me the story, and then when I could not think of any way that the outcome could have been changed, he stated that the mother could have stepped in front of the car. Yes, she would have been injured, but her daughter would have survived. I told him that there was no way I could have seen that as a path to choose. There was a moment of silence, and then he said, *"You may not have thought it now, but you did it, you did it, on the roadway, in 1981."*

Things happen, events unfurl, as we move down the hallway of life. I have walked the hallway and have opened each and every door that I have encountered, it seems, to see what is available on the other side, to seek new opportunities, and to achieve some magnitude of success. I felt that I carried the torch for my family and that if God would only permit it, and if I believed it enough, I could change the future. I begged for help to win the Powerball lottery and with those winnings ensure the comfort of my family for the remainder of their lives. Realizing that I may not be able to believe enough, I struggled to change my life, seeking new job opportunities and continuing my education. Still, no matter how hard I worked, no matter how my salary grew, it was never enough. I became obsessed with the idea of gaining wealth and looked harder at each door that could lead to instant riches. I played lottery games constantly; each time I saw a lottery sign, I would stop and buy a ticket, like opening a door to see the instant wealth inside. The result each time was an empty room, so I would go on down the hall, wishing and praying for a miracle to occur as I continued to open each and every door.

MESSAGES

In the spring of 2009, while driving to work, the date of August 28 came to my mind along with a set of instructions.

> *I have a thought as I drive past a local gas station and see the value of the next Powerball drawing posted in the window.*
>
> *"August 28. On August 28, you will purchase these numbers and only these numbers, you will play no other numbers. The numbers are: (I write down five numbers in sequence along with the sixth Powerball number.) You will pick these numbers on this day. You will play these numbers and only these numbers, no other numbers shall you play."*

The instructions were very clear in my mind. That on August 28, I would select the Powerball numbers, the numbers that were presented and that I had written down. That I would play these numbers and these numbers only, no other numbers would I play. I was to buy these numbers on August 28 and no other day.

I thought deeply about the numbers that I had been given. Looking back, I reviewed what I did for each and every month. I always played the same set of numbers that I had derived myself. Diligently, each month, I would fill out my card and submit it for advance plays that would cover the entire month. On top of this, each time I stopped for gas or walked into a grocery or convenience store, I would imagine that I was there for a purpose and that I needed to buy a Powerball or lottery ticket. I had a tracking worksheet on my computer where every month or so, I would check all the winning numbers for each week and then I would take the tickets where I had won a few dollars in to receive my cash. Generally I would purchase more quick picks or the next month's plays with those winnings. Needless to say, I lost more than I won, but I felt that when God decided it was time for me to win, it would happen. Toward the latter, each day I prayed that this gift would be given, and I created another worksheet that provided the distribution of the winnings, my children and my brothers each getting their share.

Having received the message above, I started following those instructions to the letter. I did not purchase another ticket but awaited the date of August 28. Still, I worried if I had heard the numbers correctly; did I write the correct sequence down? I needed confirmation.

The information was all related to the Powerball drawing, the numbers that I would select, and the date that I would make this selection, August 28. I asked Rich to meditate on this date; providing no additional information, I asked him to tell me the significance of August 28. A few days later I called him, we talked for a while, and then I asked if he had thought about the date. He told me that he had asked the question and that he had a message for me.

He was given the choice of delivering the message or letting "him" give me the message. His response was that he would rather not deliver the message himself, but preferred that "he" provide the response. It was at this point, while driving down the road, talking on a cell phone with him, that the conversation with him abruptly changed and I began speaking with someone else. I trembled inside as I heard these words and received the following explanation:

> *There were several seconds of silence, then a deep breath was taken.*
>
> *Me: Are you there? (talking to Rich)*
>
> *He: Yes.*
>
> *Me: (Realizing that there was something different, someone different, the voice is low, raspy) What is your name?*
>
> *He: I am known by many names.*

Me: What may I call you?

He: Zophiel. The Powerball sequence 8–2–8. This is an angelic numerical sequence. A part of life, a part of what we do. (I struggle to hear) 8 = death/birth, 2= flesh/spirit, 828 a transition sequence of spirit to flesh or flesh to spirit.

Me: Zophiel (I am having a hard time hearing, his voice is raspy and it is over a cell phone), I think I heard the Powerball sequence 8–2–8, death, flesh to spirit, death.

He: The Powerball sequence 8–2–8, death and birth, flesh and spirit, birth and death, it is an angelic sequence. It is a metamorphosis, like the caterpillar to a butterfly, the maggot to a fly. It is a transition. We all experience transitions. Do you understand?

Me: I think I do.

He: Don't think, thinking is superficial, only skin deep, on the surface; it does not reach to the soul. Accept.

Me: (At this point I begin feeling selfish, I was talking to an archangel, my thoughts turned to my son and his daily suffering.) How may I help him?

He: Do nothing. Give him comfort and love. All that he has is all that he needs spiritually; he is where he is supposed to be. 828, the Powerball sequence, it is about transitions. You and Mimi make your own transitions. Transitions occur, but they only occur if you want them to.

I must admit that more was said, but I captured these direct words in my notes. Again, I was driving down the road, during part of the conversation, taking notes on a sheet of paper on my console, and then finally stopping the truck and listening intently as I struggled to curtail my excitement and curiosity. This was the first time that I spoke directly to anyone like him, an archangel, one of God's highest messengers. If you have never had such an experience, you cannot even begin to understand the impact on your life. I cannot see how I am worthy enough to have had such an experience, such a blessing bestowed upon me, yet I did receive that beautiful communication, and I continue to thank God and him for this precious gift and the many gifts that followed. It has led to my continuing effort to adjust my life, my actions, and my words. As a quick aside, I use the word "gifts" for what I have received, but this is not to be interpreted as a physical possession. It goes much deeper.

To return to that moment in August of 2009, my thoughts were filled with the vision of the riches that were about to be bestowed upon me. My prayers were finally answered. Those thoughts filled by mind and fed my greed. I struggled for verification that I had heard the directions correctly. I begged for confirmation. I summarized the conversation with my son and told him about the confirmation I had received regarding the date and the Powerball numbers that I had received that day driving down the road. He listened to this explanation and told me that he was confused. He stated that it did not make sense, why would they give me the numbers to the Powerball lottery drawing? Wealth was not a gift to expect, it is too superficial. Yet, the words that had been spoken directly to me, over that cell phone that subsequent morning, were from an archangel, one of the masters of universal knowledge, the highest of God's messengers, and those words acknowledged that I had heard the direction correctly in my mind. I had told no one that the thoughts were more than August 28 and that the Powerball numbers were involved, and the first words spoken by Zophiel were acknowledgment of the message. *"The Powerball sequence 8–2–8."*

I continued routine conversations with Rich; we spoke of many things, among them, whether I had received the correct information and whether I was on the correct path. He asked them and then he told me that they laugh softly as they watch me on my morning walks with my hound dog:

> They said, *"Look at him; he believes it enough to follow the directions exactly, yet he still needs confirmation."*

> To me they said, *"Your message is true; why would we deceive you?"*

I followed the direction so exactly at first; I thought I must do so because if I swayed one way or another, that I would not be given the riches promised. Later I would discover the impact of receiving information of this magnitude that could change so much, so quickly. Yes, it was there, the information was correct, yet the true nature of the direction given and the difference between superficial desire and thoughts as compared to universal messages and spiritual evolution would need to be understood.

I think today that I understand that there are soul-level requests to God that are answered by his messengers. They are the messengers, delivering a response to the soul's true desire. God does not directly respond to any request but instead lets you know that he exists and that he loves you unconditionally. His response to you is always the same. He loves you! What happens beyond that is up to you. You can make changes in your life if you have the desire to do so. That desire, coupled with the application of energy and commitment, can make a difference. I like to think that it has made a difference for me, in the way I think and feel. No, I admit without hesitation that every day has failures. But I have pledged to myself and them that I will continue to try. I will try because I believe without a doubt in God and the gift of life that he has given me. I understand angelic gifts, how the appointed messengers of God may assist me in my everyday life. I understand the roles of spirit guides and guardian angels. I feel them around me every day. I still have my ups and downs and sometimes hurt more deeply than I have ever hurt. It is a penetrating hurt, a hurt that pierces the heart, but then disappears when I raise my head to God and acknowledge his love.

This hurt was amplified on the morning of January 29, 2011, when I received a call from the veterinarian's office. My hound dog had died the previous night. The doctor explained to me what had occurred; I responded to her questions the best I could and then told her I could not talk anymore. I reviewed everything that had happened over the last several hours. I could not explain it very well, but I understood; she was a blood hound, she loved the family, as God and the angels love each of us. That they would love us so much that they would choose to take my dog from me, you may not understand. For me, I loved her deeply, as did my wife, I miss her so much and still mourn her passing. Despite my tears, despite my tortured heart, it is so clear to me, she passed on to protect the family, and they chose to take her for the family.

Later I will tell you a story about the two angels. For the moment, consider the option that everything may not be as it seems. God's blessings are not always evident, but they are there and they are eternal. If you have not already done so, may you discover God's continuous blessings, may you feel his presence and his infinite love.

A JOURNEY

I sometimes think about the meaning of life. For me, life is about choices; some are in line with my life's plan, and others may be tangential to that plan. I struggle to understand those choices and to separate what I should do from what I should not. My general belief is, if it doesn't feel right, then it probably isn't. Sometimes I set goals and objectives for myself that I cannot achieve and then become discouraged by the outcome. Other times I set my goals too low, and once again I become discouraged by my own lack of achievement. If I become despondent enough, I may begin to blame others for my predicament. After all, it is easier to blame others than recognize my own mistakes. However, to understand choice implies an understanding that I am in control of what happens to me in my life. If I am in control, then that has another implication, the implication that I have the ability to change the way things are or the way they appear.

To change, I must first understand where I am and then know where I desire to be. After that, change comes from the expenditure of energy, the energy that is required to move from one point to another. Without that application of energy, I will not move forward. That does not mean that movement is impossible, as I can move. The question is, move to where? The metamorphic path from which I have come is already paved; it is all downhill. I must expend energy to maintain my current position, and additional energy is required to move forward. If I do not expend that energy, then I will be pulled (gravitationally) back from whence I have come. To do nothing means I regress. To apply energy, I must not only have the desire for change, but I must also be willing to apply the necessary energy for that change to take place. Yet, all of the desire and ability to apply energy will still not

27

move me in the correct direction if I don't know where I am and where I should go. If I know not where I am, I am just a lost soul, searching for something but not knowing what, or where to find it, wandering around, hoping by chance something magical will occur and that I will arrive at some desired destination by circumstance; ironically, that circumstance may be the true destination, or a sufficient destination for me to achieve in this lifetime. For unto God, nothing that I would do would be wrong.

My physical life started in 1954, when I returned to this world once again. My father stood outside the nursery and looked at me, his fourth son. He was a proud father, but he worried about the future. A man approached and gazed upon the newborn infant boy. "You have so many sons," he said to my father, "and I have none, you are so fortunate." I suppose that my father might have replied something like, "Yes, but I also have the hospital bill to pay and the cost of raising these boys." It would not have been something to complain of, but just a part of his pride in his sons and the fact that he could take care of all of this, but not without work. Whatever the case, the man saw it as opportunity and continued, "Give me the boy, I will pay all of the bills and raise him properly." It is not clear the complete level of wrath that my father demonstrated at this moment, but suffice it to say the man hurried away with no further attempt to acquire the boy.

This story reveals many things about my childhood and explains a lot about my philosophy today. First, I consider myself feudalistic. There is nothing in this world more important than family. I may have struggles with my family, but those struggles are for us to resolve, internally. If you are a part of family, you are protected by family. My father's response to the stranger was all about the protection of family. Whatever we would experience in the future would be worked out together, as family. Next, there exists the fact that energies will manifest themselves in one form or another in an attempt to separate that family bond. In the story presented to me, it took on the manifestation of a lonely man, desiring a son and willing to pay for one. He was an outsider with no apparent understanding of the bond of family. The next part of me is my connection with God. I have struggled with my understanding of God, which has been tainted by religious training. I used "tainted" because I am not convinced that all that is published and taught via religious counsel is accurate. I am also convinced that there exist negative energies that would work to separate us from our bond to God. He holds us tightly to his essence, but realizing that we cannot be held rigidly with strict rules and guidelines, lest we rebel; he gives us freedom of choice. His love is more powerful than the family bond. It is the depth of that love that also gives us this ultimate freedom. There are no conditions, we may cause him pain by our rejection of his messages, but he will never reject us.

Once again I understand that you may reject my understanding. I would simply say that I recognize that the universe is many billions of years old, our planet is over four billion years old, and we, humankind, have only existed for ten thousand years. If I look at this with any ounce of realism, then I must recognize that we are much too young to have a full and complete understanding of either the universe or spirituality. The next point that I try to understand is that most religious philosophy was developed in the past thousand years and has generally not evolved. We have changed, but religious culture is locked in repetitive rules that require a deeper look. A bit later, I will discuss the concept of seeking knowledge or possessing knowledge. For now, let it suffice to say that I am seeking knowledge I do not possess and am therefore open to receive new information that could promote learning.

The glimpse of the early years of my life must be understood. I was the youngest of four sons. My eldest brother was six years my senior; each son afterward was separated on an average by two years. All that I knew and experienced was a function of family. My daily interaction was with my immediate family, outings were with my extended family of uncles, aunts, cousins, and grandparents. I did not know anything different, all that I experienced on a daily basis was with those who knew and loved me. Never alone, protected, always with family, strangers were not permitted to interact with me. The shroud of protection was as sturdy as the fence that surrounded our country home. "Look here, boy, this is your world, and it consists solely of family." But wait, this view was about to be shattered, I was about to be introduced to the world, first in the presence of family, and then I would start school.

My introduction to the outside world began with a short exposure to the concept that the protective barriers were not impregnable. A small hen had hatched some duck eggs in the smoke house. I was about four years old and wanted to see the new ducklings. My mother and father took us into the building to see them; I stood in front of my mother. I was wearing shorts. The small hen was upset with the sudden attention to her brood and was squawking and fluttering around. Suddenly she decided to attack, and that she did; she attacked me and flogged and pecked my legs and arms. Family watched and laughed at such a funny sight. Enter fear.

The next introduction came with a visit to the school with my brothers before my sixth birthday. It was a first for me, but the time with my third brother, George, in his second grade class went fairly well. He was a known anchor; as long as he was there, I was okay. When my eldest brother, Dan, came and took me to his sixth grade class, it was much more complicated. I was not used to being that close to him for an extended period of time, and the rigidity of the classroom caused me much discomfort. Naturally I expressed that discomfort by whining and crying. Though disappointed with me, he took me back to be with George, and when my second brother, Dave, came to take me to his fourth grade class, I would not go. Enter distrust.

My ultimate first day of school, later that summer, fared no better than this day. It was a day with strangers, left alone by family to fend for myself. Suddenly the protective barriers were dropped, and I was pushed into the world. Like being dunked into a tub of ice water, the cold shock of reality tore into the mind and heart, and I cried for hours. But it was more than just that; I discovered something new, that people knew things that I did not know. The realization came hidden with a picture storyboard. The teacher showed the pictures, which included a mouse and a grandfather's clock, and asked what they meant. A child raised his hand and when called upon stated:

Hickory Dickory Dock

The mouse ran up the clock.

The clock struck one,

The mouse ran down!

Hickory Dickory Dock

I stared at the picture, I looked at the teacher, and then at the child. How was it possible that he could see that in this picture? And when she praised him, I thought, how was this possible, there is no way I could have known this? Enter doubt of self, envy, disillusionment, and the desire for knowledge.

But the lessons were not finished. The next was more difficult yet. This lesson was about pain. It was a simple afternoon, classes proceeded and then milk was delivered to the classroom, like it was every day. On this day, I dallied and only sipped at my milk. Eventually the teacher told everyone to put their milk bottles in the milk tray. I raised my hand and told the teacher that I had not finished drinking my milk. It was strange, the next thing that happened, as she got up from her desk, stomped down the aisle to my side, and then slapped my face. I looked at her, trying to understand what had happened. I did not like the feeling. Enter anger and hate.

For being so young, the lessons were still being heaped upon me. The things I did not know were extreme. I knew I had to go to the restroom, I knew I could not leave without permission, so I held my hand in the air and squirmed and squirmed, holding tight my muscles and begging for an answer to my hand. It did not come, and I soiled my drawers, there in that seat. At that moment, the teacher looked up and asked what I needed. It was too late, but I requested to go to the restroom. I walked off, uncertain of what to do next. I had no experience in how to clean myself. Baths were given to my brothers and me by our mother. I had never soiled myself before. How was I to clean myself? I did not know the answer and went through the remainder of the day and the bus ride home soiled and stinking. Enter guilt and shame.

We moved many times in my life, and I completed most of my elementary education at the R6 Elementary School in Trenton, Missouri. In 1960, my father sold the early farm of my memories, located deep in the country, to purchase another one near Trenton. We would spend the next six years on that small eighty-acre farm. It was on this farm in 1964 that my father gave me my first award of livestock. It was here that I would sit on the hillside and create the farm of my future. Milk cows, beef cows, pigs, horses were abundant on the farm of my dreams. Enter pride.

The early 1960s had many events that pulled on my self-worth. I recall my mother being away at my grandparents' home, caring for my grandmother in her last moments on earth. My brothers and I were home alone, and my eldest brother had just slapped me around for not doing what he said when the pastor knocked on the door. He entered and told my brothers about the passing of our grandmother. I had not heard him, but he stepped into the kitchen and, seeing me crying at the kitchen sink, offered comfort: "She was better off, her pain was over." I had no clue what he meant and did not ask. Later that week, at the funeral services, I looked around and questioned my own emotions. As my cousins, brothers, aunts, and uncles wept, I looked on with mild curiosity. Why didn't I cry like them? I do not know the answer, even today. The one thing that comes to my mind, as I write this, was the words my mother told me when she came home. She said that she had worked hard to keep Grandma alive, and on multiple occasions she had struggled to bring Grandma back to life. It was on the last time that Grandma looked at her and said, "It is not bad there, there is no pain, please let me go." At five o'clock that day, my mother called her brothers to help with Grandma. They stood there, my youngest uncle talking to his aunt while the older held his mother and said, "Mom, don't go, don't go."

Unlike my mother's memories of her mother, I remember Grandma as a gentle person who adored all of her grandchildren. She would always hold them tightly and share her love. She was a large woman, in girth, not height; she could not stand or walk and suffered from many physical ailments. I felt sad for her, and her pain; perhaps that is why I did not cry: it was her desire to leave, and she was able to fulfill that desire and get away from that pain. Enter sorrow.

I recall a time, I am sure during my eighth year, that my mother sent me to the barn to get a hammer from the corn crib. Normally this would have been an easy task to perform, but unfortunately I was terrified of livestock. Yes, this is another example of the dichotomy of my life; I dreamed of owning my own farm, yet I was terrified of livestock. This particular trip was compounded by the fact that my father had put several cows in the barn, and they blocked access to the corn crib where the hammer was located. In another area of the barn, my father had unloaded a truckload of used wood; a building of some sort was torn down and my father got the wood as a part of cleaning up the area. He would stockpile the wood and then have my brothers and me remove the nails, saving both the wood and nails for reuse. He always had a plan to build something.

But I digress, back to the hammer. Evaluating the situation, needing to get the hammer, and understanding that no one could know of my fear of livestock, I devised a way to walk across the top of the lumber and then scale across the side of the corn crib with my fingers and toes in the spaces between the wood slats, open the crib door, drop into the crib, and retrieve the hammer, returning on the same path. The trip into the crib worked well, and the exit was working just as well until I slipped on top of the wood, and then, ouch, a huge rusty nail pierced through my shoe, into my instep and out the top of my foot. I stood there looking at what happened, once again evaluating alternatives. The thought came to my head not to panic but remove my foot from the nail. I pulled but it did not look like my foot would come free. I then put the claw of the hammer beneath my shoe, and as I had done before with so many pieces of wood, using the hammer, I pried my foot from the board, extracting the nail. I then walked to the house, and when I saw my mother in the kitchen, I began to cry. I think back about the calmness of my actions, the careful calculations and movements performed to extract my foot from the nail that pierced through it. I was not alone at that moment, I was not afraid. They were there with me, offering protection and guidance. What would happen would happen; it was a part of the plan. They were not there for mitigation, just to help me endure. What I did not understand then, I get a better picture of today.

In the late 1950s, my father worked construction and was away from the family farm weeks at a time. In early 1960, he took a job at a local food plant, as we relocated the home farm to Trenton. Ultimately the pull for change occurred, and in 1967, my father returned to construction, this time selling the farm and purchasing a small mobile home that he would move from town to town to be close to his current work. During the latter part of 1966, we began moving some items that we would retain after the farm was sold. My brother said he would take the horse, and we loaded her into the pickup truck. A few other items were loaded into my brother's 1965 Pontiac Tempest convertible. We put a garden tiller into the trunk and tied the lid down so it would not flap. Loaded, my brothers headed off in the pickup, and I rode in the convertible with my sister-in-law. A light rain started as we drove toward their house. At the final intersection, approximately three miles to the west of the house, we turned right to proceed up a steep hill that curved to the left. The incline of the blacktop road was fairly extreme, and the car began sliding to the left; perhaps she was giving it too much gas.

All of a sudden, a car came around the curve, heading toward us; seeing the car, she stomped on the gas and our car lurched forward and then went straight off the road and plunged over a deep ravine that paralleled the road and head on into the opposite embankment. The front of the car dropped and the back of the car lifted, and I was thrown forward, my head hitting the windshield, cracking the glass. The car was almost straight up vertical, standing on its grill, nose walking; I was certain that it would flip straight over onto its top. As I was slung from one position to another, uncertain of the outcome, the car began to twist and roll to the left. Then as it rolled, the rear of the car began to fall backward. Still twisting, the car fell backward, rolling onto its top, the hood on the opposite embankment and the trunk on the edge of the road. Cradled in the center of the ravine was the convertible top, my sister-in-law and me, neither of us hurt, only slight bruises for the experience. She asked me if I was okay, and I inquired after her. She then turned off the key and when she could not open her door, I opened my window and we crawled from the car.

As we emerged, the other passing car returned; its occupants jumped out, exclaiming disbelief that we were uninjured. They were certain that we would be dead. I have often thought about that accident. I can see the car standing on its grill, flipping forward. I can see the impending impact, sure death, when the car would complete its flip and land upside down. Then, I see the sudden change of direction, its twisting roll and final resting location. What changed its course: its momentum, the wind, the velocity vector coupled with the altered center of gravity due to the two bodies being slung around inside, or was it something divine? This thought nagged my mind for over forty years. Not daily, but it would come up and I would see that car, standing on its nose, appearing to pitch forward, then the twist and roll, landing upside down in the perfect cradle. When given the opportunity, I asked him about this event.

Me: What was it that caused the car to fall back on the bank?

He looked at me gently and pulled on his cigar.

He: Gravity.

He[4] smiled, took another pull on his cigar, and settled down into another discussion. I think about his response, a direct response to the question that was asked. I think, if I had asked who had redirected the path of the car, or if I had asked if another may have assisted, the answer may have been different. The reason I rationalize the response in this way is because of an additional understanding that I have. This understanding is that the question asked is the one that is answered; they do not answer the question you mean to ask. They are very direct; there is no ulterior motive in a response, no sense of pride or need to deceive. If you ask which of two alternate paths you should choose,

---

4   "He" refers to he that was there at the time. In this case the name or referenced identity was 113, the 113th in line for delivering a message.

they will help you identify the pros and cons of each path. They will not tell you which to choose, as you have free will; it is your choice. The purity of their communication is astounding. The understanding is often complex.

Back to the rollover; was there angelic intervention, that day on the road, as the car pitched over? The answer is yes, I knew it before I asked, and it was reaffirmed at the point that I asked the question. Why ask a question to which I already know the answer? This latter question is simpler to understand. The reason I asked the question is for confirmation. I continue to suffer from the temptation of doubt. I understand where doubt comes from; I work to clear my mind, to clear doubt. As an example, in the Book of Robes it states that Peter stood next to he that came before (Jesus), on the water. He stood with him who had no doubt, and as long as Peter was able to keep doubt from his mind, he was able to stand on the water. But, according to the biblical account, doubt entered Peter's mind, and because of that doubt, he plunged into the water. I understand human fragilities, yet to rationalize and create an excuse of the fragilities of being human for having doubt is not really appropriate, and I should not hide behind such an excuse, yet I do.

In the summer of 1967, I worked with my brothers, moving hay for the local farmers in and around Unionville, Missouri. Together we were paid five cents per bale of hay, my share being one half cent a bale. I earned a total of $50 over the summer. At the end of the summer, I took the money and purchased new clothes for school. What was important on this path was working hard and earning enough to make my own way. On the first day of the first job, there were one thousand bales of hay in the field. We started work at seven in the morning and roughly twelve hours later had moved all of the hay. During the day, due to the heat and sweat, I took off my brand new glasses and placed them on the tractor seat, while I unloaded the hay bales from the wagon and put them into the elevator that took them up into the barn, where my brothers would grab them and stack them. After the last bale was moved, I jumped down from the wagon, climbed up onto the tractor, and flopped myself into the seat. I immediately stood back up and looked at my eyeglasses there in the seat, earpiece twisted from the frame. On that day I earned five dollars. Replacing the eyeglasses cost me twenty dollars. I would basically work for more than a week for a pair of glasses.

This did not dismay me, there was no reason to think about "could have," "should have," "wish I had," as it was too late for that. What happened was that I broke my eyeglasses. The path forward was from this location, there was no going back in time. It was regrettable, forget it, learn from it, and move forward. This attitude has benefited me many times in my life. It does not mean that I should randomly move around with disregard to the outcomes, but instead to accept what happens when it happens, learn from it, try not to repeat mistakes, and move forward. I have found that when I don't know what to do, I just ask, the answer will come, I just need to listen.

We moved three times that year, and in 1968, at a mobile home park in Marshall, Missouri, I began working outside the home, picking up garbage and mowing lawns. From 1967 on, my parents never had to purchase clothing for me, perhaps except for Christmas gifts. I worked the next two years, until my sixteenth birthday, for Wilbur and Oriene, owners of the park. Wilbur was a kind man, a plumber by trade, who was not afraid of hard work. I think I earned his respect those two years because of my work ethic and determination to move forward. Oriene, on the other hand, was not as accepting, thinking that she was something of a matriarch who deserved respect and obedience due to her position as owner and employer. She would use the job as a tool to get her will obeyed, and when she offered me the opportunity to accept her will or quit, I chose the latter and moved on.

Though I have been very critical over the years about her and I took pride in the independence I expressed on the day I quit, I now understand much better that moment and what really occurred. I cannot feel disrespect toward her any more, I cannot continue to hold to the grudge I had for so many years; instead, today, I can only give thanks for the opportunities they gave to me. Wilbur has passed on, and I am sure that he has better things to do with his time, but if he sees me now, I am sure that he fully understands my true appreciation for all that he did. My father and he were very close friends for many years; I thank him still for his patience, understanding, and help. I think back on the years that I worked for them, the people I met and the thoughts I had, the actions that I took. I was duty bound to work for this man. My father had asked for work for his sons and it was offered. To honor my father, I must do the work. It was okay, I had nothing else to do, and I enjoyed having money to spend. I picked up garbage twice a week, earning five dollars for four hours of work. I had worked far more hours for less, so it was okay. This was not my lifelong dream, it was just something to do, for someone that needed help, with reasonable compensation. Yet, please understand, it was not an easy job and had many nasty moments. But I did the job, cutting grass and removing weeds during the summer months, picking up trash each and every week.

I set my sights on the future and moved forward. Beneath this effigy of loyalty was hidden a troubled mind. I struggled to escape from the darkness, the darkness that pushed me to do unthinkable acts. I suppressed most, succumbing to a few; a few too many. After my sixteenth birthday, I decided I must escape the darkness. I did not like the feeling of its power over me. I did not understand what the power was, nor did I understand what I must do or how to do it. I just knew that something was not right, and I must do something about it.

When I turned sixteen, I applied to work in grocery stores and fast food diners; I took a job as a fry cook. At the end of my first week as a fry cook, I was offered a job at a local grocery store as a "carry out," sacking groceries and carrying them to the customer's car. I was a very large boy, a little less than six feet in height but weighing over two hundred and sixty pounds. The manager was hesitant to hire me because of my size but agreed to give me a chance. The first night was very busy, and I felt that I needed to prove myself after his hesitation. It was a typical Missouri summer, hot and humid in mid-July. I was not used to the stress and moving from air-conditioning to the outside heat and back again created a drenching sweat on my body. I would rush to the water fountain for drinks as often as possible, but after four hours the expected occurred. I became violently ill, and while rushing toward the restroom, I vomited in the aisle, twice. After I cleaned myself up a bit, I sat for a while and then was sent home with instructions to come talk to the manager the next day.

The next day, the manager told me it appeared that I could not handle the job. I looked at him and asked why he would discard me after what I had done. Had I not shown my willingness to sacrifice even my personal health to get the job done, and done correctly? He just smiled and said to be back at four o'clock to continue work. After a couple of weeks working in the store, the manager called me aside again. He asked if I knew what he wanted to discuss; I said, "Yes, you are about to tell me of the raise I will receive." He smiled and asked why I thought that I would get a raise, and I explained that I worked harder than most there and that the others were all paid more than I, therefore it only made sense that I would get a raise. The meeting was over, and I received a nine-cent-per-hour increase in pay. Two other employees were terminated. I later found out that he had called me aside to terminate me too, but the confidence I had about my performance (information that was substantiated by the assistant managers and others that I worked with) changed the path that day.

Today, I understand more about what really happened during those two transitional points in my life. I needed to sustain myself and crawl from the darkness that bound me. The path was in front of me, I had to move forward to a transitional point. No, this was not my final destination, but a demarcation point, a point that would give me the foundation to survive the next transitions that were coming in my direction. God continued to look upon me with love, the same love he has for all, while my spirit guide and guardian angel stood with me, understanding my needs and giving me the words to speak and actions to perform, words that helped me stay focused on the work and the actions to perform. The results were that I continued to work there for another three years as I completed my high school education. Within this period, I did not always understand the words that were spoken, I could not hear any better than I hear and understand today. But I knew that I must do something.

It was somewhat sad to look back on those days and see myself each day driving to the municipal swimming pool and sitting in the parking lot, watching and waiting. I was fascinated with a young girl from school, but I did not know how to speak with her. She was a lifeguard there, and I would park next to her car and wait until she got off work. I only needed a couple of moments to speak with her, to explain how I felt. I could not swim, so I would not go inside the pool area, and I was terribly self-conscious and could not try anything more than what I was doing. She would get off work and walk to her car, I would say hi, she would acknowledge my presence and then leave. I would follow her down the road to her home, and I often drove by her house two or three times during the night. Yes, today we would call that stalking. I did not mean any harm and never would have done anything more than try to find a way for her to see me and know me from the heart. If I caused her any pain and worry, I am sorry. I hope she reads these words and can forgive me.

Another transition was coming; things would happen that I would not fully comprehend until much later in life.

In 1971, I was accepted by the University of Missouri, Rolla, for the fall semester of 1972. I would be the first of my family to attend a university, and I looked forward to going there. It, however, was not meant to be; another transition sequence began. First, during the latter part of 1971, I discovered that my father was having an affair. I held this information close, as I thought it might just pass on, like so many other of his extramarital activities over the years. In this case, it was not to be, and in the spring of 1972, my father and mother divorced. I watched the progression of this event, not knowing how to halt it. I spoke with my father about his ongoing affair and asked if he thought it was worth it. He only looked at me, challenging what I would know about such events, and continued down his chosen path.

Within a couple of months of the formal separation, before the actual divorce, longtime family friends introduced my mother to a divorced friend of theirs, and the path for my parents was set. Before my eighteenth birthday, my mother chose to move closer to her new gentleman friend; I moved out of the house to live on my own. At first, I stayed with a cousin, and then I rented a house with new friends. While this was occurring, I assessed my path to college. Not knowing the ins and outs of financial aid and scholarship opportunities, with much disappointment, I did not enter college in 1972 as planned, but continued to work at the grocery store. Everyone around me seemed to be watching, waiting for me to do something. I wanted more and struggled with my existence. At work, I moved from carry out to grocery stocker, my eyes on a position as assistant manager.

I tried to make the best of things alongside my new friends, all sons of broken families. We rented a house together in the summer of 1972. We worked, we had fun, and I continued to worry. Something was not right; I felt something pulling at me, something this place and this time could not satisfy. My roommates did not stay together very long; one struggled with his identity, the other looked for permanence in his life, and I struggled to leave. A series of events began that would sever the anchors that bound me to them and this small town in Missouri. First, I was dared by one of my friends to demonstrate the power of my 1969 Pontiac GTO. All that evening, I was dared to do this and that, always responding that to take the dare would be stupid, and then, I took the last dare, foolishly. The dare was to exceed a hundred miles per hour in less than a quarter mile, on a city street. I reached the speed but the end result was a wrecked car, as I slid out of control on a sharp curve, blowing out two tires on the left side of the car as it slipped across a curb. The car stayed upright but was completely destroyed beneath, its frame sprung.

The second event occurred because of seeing one of my friends, at age eighteen, sexually involved with a girl of thirteen. I convinced the others along with her to play a trick on him, where she would claim to be pregnant, a trick that he would not forgive. He would return the trick by "play attacking" me with a knife. He held the knife to my throat; I looked at him and said, "Cut if you have the nerve." This action would break the ties of our friendship, and I immediately moved out of the house into my own apartment. Though my friends and associates at work stood solidly beside me through all of this, it was not enough. I was looking for more, and my soul ached to move forward.

In the spring of 1973, life seemed empty. I had wrecked the car the winter before, I was alone, and I was struggling with my future. I sat on the front steps at my apartment and gazed toward the heavens. "Dear God, what am I to do?" I asked, probably more rhetorically than anything else. But the universe was moving forward, and my next transition was unfolding. The next day was a busy day at the grocery store; I was working at the express checkout stand. A man in uniform stepped up and stood there in front of me; he was the US Army recruiter from up the street. I had never spoken with him, not even a casual greeting. He looked at me directly and said, "What time are you coming up to talk to me?" "In about an hour," I replied. I think of this interaction and consider it one of the direct responses from God to answer my soul's cry for help. All of the anchors holding me to this small town were crumbling; the only thing left to do was take the next step forward. There is absolutely no way that I could know what would come next or the many doors that were there in front of me, awaiting my next choice. I did not have to go for an interview, but it was a choice that I needed to make.

I went to the recruiter's office that afternoon and volunteered for the US Army. I was sixty pounds overweight with high blood pressure and was initially denied. Through the summer, I followed a strict dietary program. I removed all food from my apartment and only ate at a local lunch counter and another fast food restaurant. At both of these locations, I found new lady friends. The two of them were so precious to me; their friendship asked nothing of me, but me. My self-confidence grew, as I continued to separate myself from one shell after another. Yet, even as I removed these shells, others were being overlaid in their place. Later I will talk about wall paper as a metaphor for the protective barriers or excuses I put around myself or hide behind. For now, I will just tell you that I was given many an opportunity to develop but would often get lost again and continue to hang wall paper. My struggle to lose weight was tremendous. My gluttony and desire were extreme, and although I had purged every ounce of food from my apartment, at night I rummaged through the kitchen cabinets and refrigerator, seeking any single morsel that I may have overlooked. There was none. Although I could not halt myself from looking, I could keep myself from leaving the apartment to find something to satisfy my hunger. With extreme effort, I held to my plan, and on July 2, 1973, I had lost forty pounds and was finally accepted into the Army.

My initial time in the Army was spent in the hospital at Fort Leonard Wood, Missouri, where I was on a six-hundred-calorie-a-day diet. After dropping twenty more pounds, I started my Army basic training course. Army basic infantry training was interesting, hard but interesting. I met new people, had new experiences. I walked into the barracks one Saturday afternoon and saw a couple of soldiers holding a bag of crumpled weeds that looked like sage. I realized it was marijuana. They looked at me and said nothing; I focused on my own responsibilities. Later that night, outside the barracks, they confronted me, in an effort to scare me away from the thoughts of talking. I felt alone, uncertain of what would happen next, when another man stepped up next to me. This man was a loner, I had served guard duty with him one night, and we talked about ourselves; I asked him many questions about where he had been and why now he chose to join the Army. Now, here in the dark, he stepped between my intended assailants and me. "You will have to get through me before you get to him," he quietly told the group. "We have no quarrel with you," they replied. He responded, "He is my friend, and if you have a quarrel with him, then you have a quarrel with me." They looked at him and then replied, "We have no quarrel with him." At which point they walked away. This quiet, calm man then turned to me and said, "Be careful, don't go out alone into the night, you never know what you will come up against, there will not always be someone available to help." I studied him for a moment and then said, "You were walking out here alone." He simply nodded and then walked away.

This did not completely end the harassment, and to be honest, I probably deserved whatever came my way. I was still uncertain about myself and struggled to stand up on my own. I discovered that I was afraid of more than livestock, but like my previous fears, these also needed to be suppressed. All I really needed to do was create a shell around myself and continue to cover up whatever issue arose. I considered it part of growing up. Often when asked where I come from, I state that I was born and raised in the countryside of north-central Missouri and grew up in the Army. I graduated from Army basic training in the fall of 1973 and moved on to my advanced Army training in Fort Gordon, Georgia. Another transition was about to begin.

The next event could be characterized as one of the most consequential spiritual transitions of my early years. This event occurred during Thanksgiving weekend of 1973. My friends and I were short of money and decided to go off the post into Augusta, Georgia, to sell a pint of blood at a local blood center. I had not been eating well and was drinking too much. I barely passed the blood check, and then, being the first time that I had ever had blood drawn in this fashion, kept my fist tight from the moment the needle was inserted into my arm until the pint bag was filled. When I called the nurse to check the bag, she commented it was the fastest she had ever seen anyone fill a blood bag; she sat me up, handed me twenty dollars (which I put into my shirt pocket), and then I passed out. I was brought around with an ammonia inhaler and then was sent into another room where I lay down to recover. As I sat there, my head began to feel light, and I grew nauseated. Trying to clear my head, I lay down on the floor and put my feet up onto the chair to increase the blood flow to my brain. Shortly afterward, I felt myself drift off, and then I left my body and fell deep into darkness. Down through the darkness I descended, quickly at first and then slowly. I struggled to stop my descent, and finally I hovered. When I stopped, I looked deeply into the shadows, struggling to see. There was someone there, and they began calling me.

They: Richard, come join us, we are waiting for you.

I thought one of the voices sounded like my paternal grandmother, but why would she be there? She was alive and well.

Me: No, it is not time, I must go back.

Despite their objections and continued calls, I struggled hard and began to rise. Slowly I ascended back from where I had fallen, and then I opened my eyes. I looked around and saw someone there looking at me; I asked for help. He did not respond. I struggled to speak, to request help again, but it was like talking out loud in your sleep. You want to speak but no sound comes out. I struggled, and then with a great deal of effort, I said, "Get the nurse." He did not respond. Again I struggled and said, "Get the nurse." He got up and went out of my sight while I lay there on the floor. The nurse came to my side and took my vital signs. I could see that she was somewhat nervous as she felt for my pulse and then checked my blood pressure. She turned and requested some assistance from others in the room. "Help me get him to the car," she said. I looked at her and asked, "What is the matter, what do you want to do?" She stared at me and said that she needed to get me to her car so that she could take me to the emergency room. I said, "Okay, let me get up." As she continued to stare at me, I slowly stood and said, "Let's go," and I walked toward the door. My friend had just finished giving blood and asked me what was happening. I smiled and said, "I have gotten us a ride back to the post."

As we drove, she continued to glance at me, and at the hospital I overhead her tell them that she brought me there because I had sold a pint of blood and that the blood draw was so fast that I had passed out twice; when she check for vital signs, she had been unable to find a pulse and could not get a reading on my blood pressure. I was held in the hospital emergency room for about two hours, while the doctors and nurses monitored my blood pressure. My strength slowly returned, and I was released with strict instructions to get something to eat, stay away from alcohol for a couple of days, and rest.

The events that transpired that day were important to my understanding of the spiritual world, but I would set it aside for many years. It was too inconvenient then for me to think about all that happened and to make sense of what occurred. It was best to set it aside. I don't think that was the wrong decision. I doubt that I could achieve what I needed to achieve if I had lingered on what had occurred. I was reminded recently that it is necessary to live one life at a time. During this life, focus on the objectives of this life, strive for the perfection that was put into the plan. Personal focus is important, listen to the inner self, what we call our conscious. When something is right, it is understood; when something is wrong for us, that is also understood. Too often the inner voices are ignored.

I initially joined the US Army on a two-year program, intending to go to college after that. During processing at Fort Leonard Wood, I was given an opportunity to extend my enlistment to get guaranteed military training. I did so and then selected a duty station in Germany. I looked forward to the assignment, but during the last weeks of training at Fort Gordon, I was recruited for classified work, and my first duty station was changed from Germany to the Republic of Korea.

Let's take a moment and look at the series of events:

1. *College plans*
2. *Parents' divorce*
3. *On my own*
4. *Wreck car*
5. *Cry for help*
6. *Meet with recruiter*
7. *School guarantee*
8. *Out of body experience*
9. *Classified assignment*
10. *Duty station: Korea*

On another side of the ocean, other events were occurring. These were the events of Mimi, my future wife. Her life was in turmoil: struggling with the future, battling family issues, feeling rejected and abandoned. Her friend asked her to work for her one day; I had just arrived in the country, and my new boss took me downtown to show me around. She and I met on that day, standing there, face to face, drawn by something more powerful than life. I am certain that I recognized her that day, and the love I have for her now is undiminished from the love I had for her then, but I did not yet realize it. It was very hard to establish the relationship and bond that we have together. It was often just as hard to maintain that relationship. Negative thoughts and distrust pushed their way into our world, constantly trying to disrupt the life we share. In the past, we would fight against each other so hard; it hurts to think about it. Words were said, accusations were made, then the defense, the justifications, the excuses, counter blame and counterattacks. We fed the negative energies, and the more we reacted, the stronger those energies became. How could I have fought with someone that I love so much? It does not make sense when looking back; it would set the stage for things to come.

The first year we were together, our son Richie was born. Two years later, our daughter Sissy arrived to complete our family nest. Mimi has an older half-brother, a full brother by her mother, a few years senior to her, two half-brothers, and a stepsister. Her mother died of a burst appendix shortly after her birth. Her grandmother found her stricken daughter, holding the new baby to her breast, having passed many hours before. I am very aware that she and her mother watch over the lineage that they created, one daughter after another, each day. I will not talk much more about this, as that is a story for her to tell if she chooses. The meaning for me is that without these events that moved her on a path that would intersect mine, we would not be where we are today.

Sidebar: We were at the birthday party of my granddaughter. Rich was in a very relaxed state, tending a pork roast that was smoking on the grill, sipping a beer. As I sat with him, I observed him talking to children at the party, calling them by their names, though he had never met them before. He looked at me and told me that his grandmother was there, using the appropriate Korean title. Here is an excerpt of a discussion between Rich and his maternal grandmother:

> Her: *"Given the choice that if I had this baby, I would die,*
> *I would not change a thing, I would choose to have the baby*
> *again. Look at them, they are all so alike, just like me."*

I spent the next twelve years in the Army, with assignments in the Republic of Korea; Fort Sill, Oklahoma; and Fort Riley, Kansas. It was during my first assignment in Korea that I met and married Mimi. As of this writing, Sissy has two children. Rich and his wife are expecting their first child this fall. During the time in the Army, I struggled to be the best that I could be, always learning, always trying to find ways to attend college to achieve my childhood dreams for a formal education. I took courses at Kansas State University, Cameron University, and Los Angeles Community College. I took the College Level Examination Program (CLEP) tests to add to my résumé and college transcript, enhancing my ability to be promoted.

Take a close look at that paragraph, and you should be able to see the source of a lot of issues. Yes, there are a lot of I's.

Our life in the mid to late seventies was complex. I struggled with my own identity, full of hatred, pride, and jealousy. In 1976, Mimi, Richie, and I left Korea. She had also struggled with her family. They were concerned about her future and perhaps felt betrayed by her, given her choice to marry from outside their culture. She tells of conversations with her paternal grandmother, who always chastised her, claiming that she would never find a husband in Korea, that only a "Yankee" would want her. Whether or not she was courted by Korean gentlemen, I have no idea. But for the latter part, this "Yankee" did want to enjoy a life with her, and she decided that this relationship was good enough to leave family, marry, and follow her husband into a new life.

Mimi held tightly her closest feelings. Rarely have I been allowed to see inside those thoughts. Financial difficulties always plagued us, there was never enough money to go around. We kept a roof over our heads, the children were fed, but there was always a need for more. One morning at my father's house back in the United States, she confided to me that she had had many potential relationships. Those around her, close friends and confidants, encouraged her to be with me. She had decided to do so because she "felt sorry" for me. The conversation was one of the most difficult that I had ever endured. I had sought from her the complete love that I perceived I gave to her, yet she paid me back with this hurt. They were not the words to hear for someone already uncertain of where he fit in the picture of life; it only drove deeper levels of resentment and jealousy.

To move forward, I attempted to bury the thoughts and memories of her words, "hanging more wall paper." I began to work on the superficial shells that covered me, to create an image of toughness, strength, and courage. When I look back at this time, I see the pain that I created in our lives, the hurt that was carried, and the love that was given by her to me but never received. My wife's expressions of love were presented in actions, not words. I did not understand this part; I had not experienced this type of approach. She on the other hand understood that words were something that had no meaning without action to support them, but that actions could stand on their own; actions do not need words, but words need actions.

Let me provide an example. I can say that I love you and cherish your existence. Then after saying those words, I can go sit down and watch television while you work. I could say those words and then go out with friends to a night club and dance and chase other women. I could say those words and then scream at your, beat you, look at you with disgust. I could speak those words and then make you feel alone. You would care for the children, be up all hours of the night to check on them, to tuck them in, caress their brow, and kiss them gently. While you did all of this, I could say that you were a mean mother.

The latter thoughts were driven by the emotional extremes she would express outwardly, leaving me to feel both the physical and emotional impacts of those extremes. To look back on that time now, I can only think of how foolish I was, but that path taken was part of this journey to understanding, to arrive at this place with our children and grandchildren, all with deep love for one another, and for that reason and that reason alone, I would not change a single moment of any day. But if we could have arrived at the same place without the pain, that would have been much preferred to the former, and I would change it all if I could. Let it be clear: the end does not justify the means. I regret completely the pain that I have inflicted on those I love; I regret every harsh word ever spoken, every painful swing of the fist or hand in punishment or retribution. I do not understand the ways of the universe and the cause and effects that occur, but I think that we could not have gotten here without the joys, the love, the struggle, the hurt, and the pain, and therefore to think that I would change the past does not make sense. I can say, though, that I am truly sorry for that which resulted in pain.

I understand today so much more than I did yesterday, and today I know more of how much I do not understand about the universe. I gaze into the heavens, stare for hours at the pictures of stars and galaxies taken from orbiting telescopes. What we see is so vast; to understand it all is impossible. The age of the universe is unknown, but some have stated that the age of the earth is more than four billion years. If the current lineage of man is only ten thousand years, then we are only at the age of conception in terms of the universe. How could we expect to know even one billionth of the information available us? To possess that level of knowledge is just incomprehensible. Try to imagine and understand the physical and spiritual nature of ourselves and the complex web of interactions from person to person, thought to thought, words spoken and actions taken. I try to understand that any change, no matter how small, can have far-reaching effects across time eternal. For this understanding, I know that I must take care, to be careful of what I say and do, as it can have an impact that I would not dream, desire, understand, see, or imagine. I cannot tell you what you should do, I can only tell you what I have done and what I am trying so carefully to accomplish. Later I will write about my special fast; even the act of following my fast impacts others. It is so important, I cannot waiver, I ask God for strength and courage. The way back to where I was is paved and downhill, how easily to lose hold and fall.

Back to the journey: the complexities of our lives continued, we returned to Korea in 1977, and in 1979, I was transferred to Fort Riley, nestled in the hills of Kansas, between Junction City and Manhattan. I learned a lot there. There was much to experience, much to gain from this short time of our lives. I dove into my work, once again struggling to establish myself in new surroundings. The military organization had huge internal problems. It operated under the guise of favoritism and prejudice. Most soldiers just strived to survive, while others were on constant attack against those who were not a part of the establishment. On the day of my arrival, a young staff sergeant gave me the single most important words of advice that he could offer in regard to my unit: "Keep your back against the wall, trust no one, you are not one of them, they will attack you."

I did as he advised, always keeping myself prepared for the unexpected. I established ethical principles of behavior. First was honesty; second, integrity; and third, justice. I did not ask anyone to do anything that I was not willing to do, and I pushed training and preparedness on my team. I had many failures, make no mistake about that, but at the end of fifteen months, on the day I departed, a young female soldier stopped me in the barracks hallway, crying. I asked her what was the problem, and she said that she hated to see me leave. I challenged her claim, saying, "You don't even like me." Her response was interesting, in that it showed that my endeavors had in fact had some level of success. She said to me, "Yes, I do think you are a bastard, but you are a consistent bastard and you are fair to everyone, and that makes all the difference. No other leader here can stand next to you, and that is why I hate to see you go." But go I did, and in 1980, my family and I once again returned to my wife's homeland of Korea.

During that same time, the young staff sergeant that spoke to me had a tragic event in his life. His young daughters were killed in a house fire. I saw him a few years later; looking him in the eyes, I could see his pain, suffering, and self-blame. There was not a lot that could be said. I put my hand on his shoulder, said it was good to see him, and then walked on. As I went down the hall, I approached others that mocked me for the friendship I showed this man that they considered a loser. I told them only that they should not judge unless they were willing to walk in another's shoes. His pain is real, the result of the suffering from losing his daughters, suffering so extreme, even alcohol could not deaden the senses. I told them that the fact that he is here, performing at all, is testimony to his strength. I would hope that he finds this book and realizes that God loves him, that perhaps his girls look on him today and smile with the understanding of his deep love for them and encourage him to learn to forgive himself, if he has not already done so.

In 1981, I was chosen as a curriculum designer at Fort Sill, Oklahoma, Field Artillery School; during that time, I applied three separate times to the Army Officer Candidate School, each time failing to be selected by the Department of the Army Selection Board. Once again I thought the universe was lining up against me, that although I gave my all, it was never enough. The universe responded, and then the colonel sent for me. In his office, he acknowledged my attempt to become an officer and then pointed out another path that I could follow. If I were to accept a position as a key instructor for one of the Army's new programs, I would be on a clear path to becoming a warrant officer. I quickly agreed, and the next physical transition began to unfold. This path led to my next assignment as an instructor. There I established myself as a strong technical leader and expert in the operational aspect of the program. This work was enough to attract the attention of the prime contractor for the program when I announced my intention to leave the Army. With the future in mind, I exited the Army in 1985 to start a career with that contractor. This transition from the Army to civilian life was also a special event.

In 1983, when I had just changed jobs to become an instructor at Fort Sill, Mimi and I struggled with our marriage. She was working as a bartender and came home late every night. I was extremely jealous and could not understand why she was so late coming home each night, and when she arrived, she would lie down on the couch instead of coming to our bed. I argued with her, and she walked out of the house. When we separated, I was not sure of the path I was to take. The next two years were very difficult; after a few months of separation, we came together again for a brief period. In the fall of 1984, knowing that something was about to happen, I sought assistance from the Army mental hygiene office. I explained to them about the dark energies that were surrounding me, but after a few sessions, I was sent away with no further counseling required. A few days later, I beat her up in a drunken, jealous rage, and we divorced.

In 1985, as a single parent, I was sure that I was meant to get out of the Army; I had spoken to several people about different opportunities. I had also applied for a position with the contractor but had not heard from anyone. A series of events began to unfold; it seems strange to recall them now, but they led to my direct interaction with the key decision makers for the contractor, and when they heard of my decision to leave the Army, I was immediately hired.

Mimi and I began rebuilding our relationship at the end of 1985, and I gave her custody of the children, bought her a car, and then went off to work in my new job. A few months later, we moved to Texas and remarried; in January 1988, we moved to California. It was during the time of 1988 to 1993 that I worked to learn, both for my career and for my formal education. While working full time, often sixty or more hours per week, I also attended college on a near full-time basis, first at San Jose University, then at the University of Colorado, Colorado Springs, and finally at Regis University in Colorado, where I completed a bachelor's degree in computer science in 1993. Also in 1993, my wife started a business, cleaning homes. I worked weekends helping her, and we prepared our children for college. In 1995, I started a master's degree program at Colorado Technical College, graduating in December 1996. During this time, several transitional events occurred.

AN ACCIDENT

My son, Rich, had a head-on vehicle accident in June of 1995 that resulted in a closed head injury. This injury would take years to heal, his daily pain was tremendous, and he suffered from bulimia and anorexia. Later I will expand more on the results of this accident. In early 1996, he went out with a few friends and then came home; Sissy came and asked me if I had seen him; I said no. She told me he was dying and that I must do something. I went to his room to find him skinny, weak, his skin yellowish. Against his will and with the help of one of his friends, I took him to the hospital. The emergency room doctor explained that since he was an adult, I had no legal standing to insist on his care. I told the doctor that Rich was suffering from a closed head injury and if he could not help, then get out of the way so I could find someone that would. To save his life meant everything to me, and that is what we did.

It is not easy to bring someone back and restore their belief in themselves. It all happened one day at a time, one moment followed by another. One day, we were in my father's hospital room. He could barely breathe, having lost most of his lung capacity to pulmonary fibrosis. Rich was sleeping in a chair calmly, without the torment that he generally experienced. As I walked into the room, my father motioned me over to his side and whispered that he needed to teach Rich how to fight. I looked at my father and said he already knows how to fight, whereupon my father just shook his head and closed his eyes.

Later, as we drove home, Rich told me that he wanted to trade places with his grandfather. He said it would satisfy both their needs: his grandfather's need for a young body and his need to die. I told him this was not an option, it was not acceptable. I did not understand why he would suggest such a thing, nor did I know about the negative forces that attacked him on a daily basis. I did not know the deals that were made, the information passed, until much later. What I did know was that he was suffering, and I vowed to help him with every ounce of energy I could muster. I had no idea of the depth of that torment. I pulled toward God, and when I was introduced to Cyd, a spiritual consultant, I began frequent contact with her and continue doing so even today. This torment in his life would continue for thirteen years.

THE GUARDIAN ANGEL

Events and transitions occur independent of our recognition of them. Like the cogs and sprockets of a watch, time elements rotate until a position is reached, and then something happens. In this instance, in the fall of 1995, my wife had taken on a new cleaning contract at a local funeral home. Several times a week and on weekends, she would take a crew into the facility to clean the offices, presentation rooms, mausoleum, and chapel. Our daughter was home from college for a weekend visit and went to see her mother; she walked into the chapel on a Sunday afternoon. She looked around for her mother and then saw something unusual. Floating in the air over the head of one of her mother's employees, who was cleaning the chapel area, was a physical apparition. Upon seeing this apparition, she immediately turned and ran from the building and would not return. Two days later, driving north back to college, she fell asleep behind the wheel of her car. Her car left the highway and went into the dirt median. She awoke, saw a bridge abutment, and tried to regain control of the vehicle. At this point, a voice in her head told her, "Go back to sleep; everything will be okay." She released her hold on the wheel, closed her eyes, and went back to sleep. She woke to the sounds of men trying to remove her from her vehicle, which had been totaled and was now facing south in the southbound lane.

Late that night, our phone rang. Her mother answered and let out a scream, and then she rushed into the bedroom and gave me the phone. Sissy was on the phone; she had taken the phone from the nurse who had just spoke to Mimi. The first words I heard from Sissy were that

54

she was okay, but she had rolled the car. I found out where she was, and we departed immediately to be by her side. She was treated for a gash in her head and released. I am confident, without a doubt, that the image she saw that day in the chapel was an angel, perhaps her own guardian angel, that showed herself to our daughter so that she would be prepared for what was about to happen. The path toward the accident was set in motion; nothing we could do would change the outcome.

I learned more about this later, in October of 2009, during another accident that did not involve our family; I will discuss that event later, but at the time of this event, I knew that my daughter survived this accident because it was a part of the plan to survive. To survive meant that assistance was needed, and it was given.

LESSONS FROM MY FATHER

In April 1996, my father passed; I mourned his passing for two years. One day, two years after his passing, I was having a harder time than usual. I was shaving in the bathroom, when the thoughts of my father's passing filled my mind, and I began to weep. I blamed myself for not being with him; I had left the hospital the day before his passing without talking to him. I had a long drive home, and the nurses were taking a lot of time cleaning him up that morning. I had stopped in his room and told him that I was going to speak with my stepmother and aunt and then come back to talk to him. Standing in the hall, I changed my mind and decided to leave and give him a call after getting home; his doctor had said he would be okay, and they were thinking about moving him to long-term care. It was all justification for leaving, and now I blamed myself, as that next morning I received a call saying that he had pulled his oxygen mask from his face and had passed. I stood there, thinking about that moment, and wept. After a moment I regained my composure and got dressed for work; the phone rang.

It was Sissy, calling from college in Fort Collins, Colorado. She was crying. I asked her what was wrong. She explained that she had had a dream; she was talking with friends when an old pickup pulled up near them. Her friends saw an old man getting out of the truck and began to laugh at him; she immediately recognized him, saying, "Grandpa!"

He approached her in her dream and told her how proud he was of her. He then asked her to tell her father and brother to let go. He said he could not accomplish what he needed to accomplish as long as we held him. I told her of my emotional breakdown a moment before and then asked if she knew of her brother's mourning. She said he had never spoken of it. I called him on my way to work, and when I asked him if he still grieved for his grandfather, he immediately broke down and wept. We discussed his sister's dream and we both agreed to let go.

THE CLAIRVOYANT

In January 2011, I watched as she sat there, looking at him, listening intently to his words. Tears came to her eyes, a smile was on her face. I could feel the energy all around us. He spoke, she said she understood.

Holy Bible, NIV, Deuteronomy 18:14–22

> *The nations you will dispossess listen to those who practice sorcery or divination. But as for you, the Lord your God has not permitted you to do so. The Lord your God will raise up for you a prophet like me from among your own brothers. You must listen to him. For this is what you asked of the Lord your God at Horeb on the day of the assembly when you said, "Let us not hear the voice of the Lord our God nor see this great fire anymore, or we will die."*

> *The Lord said to me: "What they say is good. I will raise up for them a prophet like you from among their brothers; I will put my words in his mouth, and he will tell them everything I command him. If anyone does not listen to my words that the prophet speaks in my name, I myself will call him to account. But a prophet who presumes to speak in my name anything I have not commanded him to say, or a prophet who speaks in the name of other gods, must be put to death." You may say to yourselves, "How can we know when a message has not been spoken by the Lord?" If what a prophet proclaims in the name of the Lord does not take place or come true, that is a message the Lord has not spoken. That prophet has spoken presumptuously. Do not be afraid of him.*

In the fall of 1999, Sissy was at work, listening to one of her favorite radio programs. The program featured an amazing woman, a recognized master clairvoyant, Cyd. Sissy was at a crossroads within her own life. She was dealing with a relationship that was ending and was uncertain about her own future, as she was trying to get into medical school. After listening to the program, her coworkers encouraged her to schedule a reading with Cyd. In the months that followed the reading, the events that Cyd said would happen began to occur. Amazed, she shared her story with her mother and me. As she recounted her experience with Cyd, she also discussed the radio show. On that show, Cyd had mentioned a building that was haunted. She had been asked to investigate the building, and when she went there, she found a young girl in an elevator. Recognizing that the child's spirit was lost, Cyd revealed that she had called upon the Archangel Gabriel to come take the child home. Her mother and I were impressed, and our daughter told us about Cyd's website, findthechildren.com. I thought of the child and the call upon Gabriel. I was amazed and intrigued; how was it possible to call upon an archangel directly, and for him to respond?

Mimi had often gone to spiritual advisors in Korea. In a couple of instances, we had scheduled psychic readings with prominent psychics, so it was not unusual that she encouraged me to schedule a reading with Cyd. I searched the website and saw that the cost of the reading was within reach, so I agreed and made an appointment.

What happened next was very unusual for me; from the moment our conversation began, I was drawn to the voice on the other end of the phone. The receptionist gave us a preview of what would come next. She told us that Cyd would give us information but she would have no recollection of the discussion; therefore, the session would be recorded. We scheduled a reading, which would last an hour; I wondered how we could possibly fill all of that time.

Sitting there that day, exchanging information, we sought to know what our children would be doing and where the future would lead us. Her voice was serene, and it warmed my heart to just sit and listen to what she had to say. She told me that I would be offered a job that would be a great opportunity. She told me the offer would include a remarkable relocation package. She described the people and the region where the office would be located, but she added that there would be a complex twist. I asked her if I would take the job, and she only responded that there would be conflicts that I would need to resolve.

I took extensive notes and reviewed them over the weeks that followed. I got a call with a job offer. The home office was on the East Coast, yet the job was in the Midwest. When I traveled to the interview, the people were great. It was good to talk to them, and when they made the job offer, it went exactly as Cyd had predicted. The job offer included a relocation package that was the best that I had ever seen, but I struggled with the decision; my wife would have to close her business, so I pushed for a higher salary than they could offer. The end result was I declined the position.

The results of this reading were so exact that I scheduled another shortly thereafter to understand what we needed to do in regard to the long commute that I made daily to work. Once again, Cyd responded with information that was amazing. She told us that we should put our house on the market and said that a buyer was already in the immediate area, but was not from the area. She stated that the closing would occur three months after we put it on the market. She said that we must be reasonable on the price but not aggressively so. Once again, the results were amazingly accurate. Our real estate agent worried that our price was too high for the area, and knowing our desire to move, she offered various options. We declined these options, as I was very certain of the outcome. However, I rethought Cyd's advice and lowered the price of the house by ten thousand dollars. The buyer made an offer immediately, and three months after putting our home on the market, we closed on it; the price surpassed the market for the area. The buyer was from California and was renting a home just up the street. She walked by the house daily and often thought how nice it would be to have it for herself. When she saw it on the market, her hopes rose, but the initial price was just out of her range. The moment we dropped the price, the house was hers.

These stories are just the introduction to the readings by this master clairvoyant. I scheduled readings with Cyd a couple of times a year.

Each time I found the time spent on the phone or in person to be very relaxing. Her ability to see was amazing, the accuracy of the information astounding. She became more than a clairvoyant to Mimi and me, she became a friend and advisor.

My experiences with Cyd, as well as my conversations with them, has solidified within me my understanding of the source of the information received; it also led me to conclude that this discussion was real and a part of God's messages to me. During one of my conversations with them, they told me that if I wanted to know the future, I should talk to the clairvoyant. In a subsequent conversation when they made reference to the clairvoyant again, I asked if they talked to Cyd, and their answer was, "Yes, though at times she does not listen." When I heard these words, I smiled. We are all human, after all, even those with psychic vision. A few days later, she asked me if they ever spoke about her, and I told her what they said. She laughed.

THE SEARCH FOR UNDERSTANDING

In January of 1997, I started the doctoral program at Colorado Technical University, and in 2002, I was conferred as a doctor of computer science.

Over the years, my son often called me to discuss the issues that constantly tormented him. Most of that story is something for him to discuss, but its impact on me was tremendous. I struggled to find ways to help him, and in the late 1990s I finally agreed, after a request from my wife, to seek a psychic to find out what the future would hold. For the first reading, my wife and I set up a telephone interview with a renowned psychic, who quickly summarized my wife's future and the future of our children. I did not pay much attention, but later in that year, we had our first conversation with Cyd, who has since become my dear friend and spiritual consultant. No, she is not the source of my many conversations, but she is the source of much of my understanding and the support structure that I have needed many times in the last several years. I often discussed what was occurring with our son, and she would remind him of God's love. In the fall of 2007, she told me that a divine gift was coming my way. I asked her what I must do to receive that gift, and she said, "Nothing, it is a gift from God, all you need to do is wait." A couple of months later, she spoke of a major transition for our son. He told me of a horrific nightmare.

He who tortured my son came and offered him everything. My son told me that he declined, saying he already has everything he needs. He who tortured him then stated that he would give him the world. My son replied that he did not want it. He who tortured him then said that he would take his wife, and with that, he grabbed her and began pulling her through the bed and through the floor; my son grabbed onto her, struggling to wrench her from his hold.

> *Cyd: Now he understands the power and has replied. He needs to ask specifically how he can start serving God. Devote and dedicate himself to God. What can he do in that service? His destiny plays out. His path must be instrumental, what is his vital part of destiny and fate? Look at termination, destiny, path. We can change outcome, outcome for greatest good. He does have a role if he can see the outcome. Why would he have the vision if he is not instrumental? They don't just give you knowledge if you are not a part of the process. They do not change the world but provide assistance in a significant way, think about how to serve. They (negative attacks) will continue if he cannot, it is not a victim role. Why did they choose him, what does he do with it? Events must be big to bring light. An example is the tragedy at Columbine. These events have a positive impact on the growth of our soul. He must look to the positive side. What is the reason the universe provides the information? Goodness only; why did they choose him? He must give his life to the light side, to serve. Recognize who he is and why they are giving this to him.*

I spoke with him about God's love and about focusing his thoughts away from the dark and toward the light, but I had no idea what this all meant until about two months later. When I look back on her words, which I wrote down, I can see clearly all that was foretold. I could not have seen it then; that is not the way it works. They are always careful of what they allow you to know, lest you try to change that which must occur. This was all too true, as I saw impending doom and struggled to stop what would happen next. It is easy to throw yourself in front of an oncoming truck, slamming your fist on the hood to gain the attention needed to stop the vehicle. It is easy to step in front of a bullet to save someone you love. It is instinctive, it is protective, but how do you stop something you cannot see, cannot feel, cannot hear? You may beg to stand in their place, but begging is not enough.

On February 2, 2009, our daughter called my wife and said that she had a weird dream, a premonition that something terrible was about to happen. My wife understands that our daughter can feel and see things, so she listened carefully and worried about the upcoming events that would impact our immediate family. She understood that the premonition would play out within three days.

On February 5, Rich called me and told me that the latest torment was the worst ever. They attacked him viciously. He cringed in pain. I was driving down a freeway in Los Angeles. We spoke for forty-five minutes. I told him to embrace God's love, to look deeply into the white light of God's radiant energy and put his faith in God. I told him that no harm could come to him if he held tightly to God. He said he wanted to fix dinner for Sumer, his wife; he was making garlic ginger chicken wings. We hung up the phone.

That evening, after I had returned home from a trip to California, I worried about the discussion I had with Rich that afternoon; then, as it was very late, I went to bed. Sissy called the next morning; it was Rich's birthday. She said that she had just talked to Sumer; Rich was in the hospital. Shortly after our conversation, he had slashed open each of his wrists.

My mind raced as I tried to piece it all together and explain to Mimi what had happened. We made travel arrangements to get to his side, and then I called Cyd and left a message about what had just occurred. A few minutes later, she called and without hesitation told me to separate the physical from the spiritual. She stated that this was an eternal soul event, that the negative energies could attack him no more, he was in the light, completely. She told me what would occur over the coming days and said I should relax and watch.

How difficult a task; my heart was so heavy. I struggled with what he had done, the visions of him there alone, the razor blades in his hands.

Sumer's rush to get home to find him there, struggling to stop the flow of blood from his wrist as she called 911 for help. I stood in his home that first night, staring at the bathtub; I knelt down and cleaned the small scattered bloodstains that remained, though Sumer had worked hard to clean it all before our arrival. I struggled to do as Cyd said; it was so hard.

At the hospital, I tried to embrace all that I heard; I witnessed things, interactions between him and other patients that I cannot describe, yet each interaction with him or observation of what he was doing was a confirmation of the information she gave to me. It would begin to help; it has made all the difference.

PHYSICAL TRANSITION

In December of 1985, when I left the Army, I weighed about 217 pounds. Over the next seventeen years, I gained over 200 pounds; at Christmas of 2002, I weighed close to 425. I say "close to," as I could not find a scale to weigh myself on. There were times that I thought to go to a truck scale to find out where I was. In 1995, I took pills to reduce weight (Redux) and dropped from 370 to 320 pounds. In 1996, I joined a fitness center with my son, as a part of assisting him on his path to recovery from bulimia, and at that time dropped from 350 to 325. I then did nothing for six years except grow in size. I suffered from sleep disorders and would often fall asleep while driving; staying awake in my college classes was often impossible. The professor in the last class of my doctoral program was so frustrated with me that she sought to fail me on the course. I had to work hard to overcome these obstacles and continue to move forward. January of 2003, at 425 pounds, my son encouraged me to join him on a diet based on the Atkins high protein diet plan. In that year, I dropped over 100 pounds, my low weight being 315. I stayed on the Atkins program for another six years, hovering around the 320 range and then starting to climb once again.

On July 31, 2009, my weight had risen again to 348 pounds. Each day, I would look into the mirror at myself and make a pledge to do something to start losing weight again. Each day, I would search through my closet for clothes that would fit, but most were just stretched to their limit. My wife looked at me with disgust, criticizing me each time my self-control failed and I pulled the mixed nuts from the pantry and gorged myself with a cup or two. I struggled to breathe; just hanging my head on my chest would result in my choking from the bunched fat. I tried to be noncaring and accept my situation, but I could not. It was at that point that I stood one morning in the front of the shower and cried out aloud, "Father, why have you not assisted me?"

The very next day, while driving to work, I received the answer to my cry for help. On that morning, I received the details of the fast that I should perform. I began my fast, and on the day that I write this section, October 2, 2010, I have lost a total of 134 pounds. I eat a fixed number of calories every two hours, six times a day. I do not eat or consume any caloric items at any other times. The fast was an angelic gift. I did not read about it, I did not consult a dietician; I did not get it from television or my doctor. It came to me as a message, and I have followed it fastidiously since.

Previous to the message of the fast, a different message was delivered for me, that if I were to observe seven sunrises, the angels would praise my name in heaven. I thought on this instruction a couple of days and then decided to try it. I checked the time of sunrise and got up early one morning and walked outside. The easterly view was blocked by other houses. Struggling to find a location to observe the sunrise, I got into my truck and drove down the street to find a location to observe the east. I found a perfect spot, parked the truck, and sat there awaiting the sunrise, but I fell asleep. A few minutes later, I awoke to see the sun had already risen, so I drove back home. I repeated this path for about a week, each day driving to the same location, most times falling asleep. After seven days, I had only observed two sunrises.

My current regime of daily walks started the following week while traveling on business. I got up early and walked outside of the hotel to observe the sunrise. Again the view was blocked, and I walked up the street, looking for a clear view of the east. I ended up walking about a quarter mile before I found it. At that time, walking just a quarter of a mile was difficult, ten minutes on the treadmill took every ounce of energy and will that I could produce. However, I had started something new, daily walks, and after I had observed seven sunrises, I decided that I would continue the walks as I really enjoyed that time outside.

Today, I walk up to four miles most mornings with my hound dog; my wife often accompanies us. Some days I choose to walk on a treadmill, if the roads are slick, and sometimes I will walk in the evening after work with Mimi, but my preference is to go outside and walk during the early morning. It is during this time of day that I walk to experience the positive energies of the morning sunrise, listen to the birds, feel the fresh air, and gaze upon all that the light illuminates. It is a special moment each and every day to experience the sounds, smells, sights, and touches of the many gifts given by God as proof of his unconditional love.

The gifts that I received are angelic gifts. The gifts come from those who watch over us, based on a soul-level request. We were at the hospital after our son's suicide attempt. The reason he made this attempt is a far deeper story of love and compassion than I can adequately tell. What I can tell you is that I called Cyd that morning, shortly after receiving my daughter's phone call, and she asked me to separate myself from the physical and realize the divine gift that was given to my son. I would not say that all such events will end in a divine gift, and I do not support such attempts. I do not think of attempted suicide as a blessing. I understand this event as something special that was started years or even possibly many lifetimes earlier; what ultimately transpired was tragic, but from his gift of his life to protect the one he loves so much, the angels would gather to his side and welcome him, surrounding him with divine glory and altering his life and making him what he is today.

I tried to request from him a little more cooperation with the doctors in the hospital room one afternoon; I challenged him about why he would do such a thing and said how he should cooperate with the doctors and give them what they needed so that they could treat him and send him home with us. He looked at me with deep emotion and swore to me that he never wanted to hurt anyone, not even himself, and that all that he was experiencing at this point was real. I held him close and asked him to help me understand. I can see that I am rushing the story of this event; it was drawn out over a period of nearly seven hours. We talked, we discussed the importance of family and God, and then, late into the evening, at the end of visiting hours, we prepared to leave. As I gave him a good night hug, he squeezed me tightly and told me to open my heart and mind on this night, and that if I could do this, come the morning, I should tell him what I experienced.

That night, I sat up in bed and asked that God give me the information that I needed to understand.

I awoke gently and raised my head to look around; what disturbed my sleep? It was dark, but I could see more clearly than I have ever experienced in the early morning darkness. It was like the room was completely moonlit. A fan stood in the corner, its motor gently whirring. As it swept to and fro, I could feel the gentle breeze brush across my skin, each hair on my arm gently waving under the air. It was quiet, quieter than I have ever heard; I could hear its silence. I lay my head down and then sat up again. I got up and walked to the bathroom and then back to the bed. I sat up in bed, looking into the morning. I could still feel the breeze of the fan and thought that my skin was more sensitive than before. It was a calming moment, completely comforting; pure is the best word that explains it. Then, from the silence, within my head, these words were spoken:

    He: "I am Sandalphon."[5]

I smiled ever so slightly, lay back down, and immediately went back to sleep. A few hours later, I awoke with music echoing through my mind. It was a Pavarotti song. Over and over, it played in my mind.

To remind you, earlier I discussed another challenge that was presented to me. As stated, it was originally a challenge presented to my daughter, perhaps a few shades different, but still the similar concept. Until I can pass this challenge, I shall not provide guidance to anyone. I will not judge anyone. I will control my perceptions and focus on only the good

---

[5]   Sandalphon is an archangel of music and musings who carries prayers to heaven. His brother is the Archangel Metatron, whose symbol is the Star of David.

of everything I see, hear, or feel. This challenge will take priority over everything in my life. No other task will be given a higher position. This challenge will take priority over my morning walks, over my fast, over the carving of my chain (I will tell you about this later), over discussions and debates. This challenge is all about learning, understanding, and patience. The details of the challenge seem fairly simple when you hear them: For thirty consecutive days, I shall not speak badly of anyone or anything. I shall not judge. I will not be cross or treat anyone or anything badly. I will not think badly of any word said to me or speak a bad word to anyone or about anyone. I will look at the good in all that I hear and see. If even so much as a tiny bug were to bite me on the thigh, I should shoo it away and give thanks to the transpired event for reminding me of how something so perceptively insignificant could have such a dramatic impact on the overall largeness of my well-being. If on any day I fail to accomplish any of these things within the scope of the challenge, the clock resets, and I am on day zero again. The purpose of this challenge could better be expressed by a quote of Lao Tzu: "One cannot reflect in streaming water; only those who know internal peace can give it to others."

I accepted this challenge, without hesitation, probably with arrogance. How simple a task, I could just breeze through this, almost like a walk in the park. Wrong!
Think again, what a beautiful challenge, so complex, yet so gentle. What appears in the mind is compassion and love, caring and giving. Such a simple challenge, how could anyone fail on so simple a task? Even as I write these words about this challenge, I feel the need to reset the clock and start my thirty days over once again. I have been working on this challenge for nine months; I have never gotten past twenty-two days after many resets. Yet, each setback has given me something new to evaluate. It is the subtleties that catch you: a person on a telephone help line that does not respond the way you desire, an airline ticket agent, a repairman, the words of an e-mail, the crying of a child, the arrogance of a fly that buzzes around my head. Each of these draw different emotions from one's self. Those emotions are fragile, they seem to bend and adjust easily, then . . . snap, they break, and the torrent of negativity fills the mind and exists in words and actions.

I watch these events that occur in front of me, I respond, I make mistakes. Each and every time, I lose my connection to what I must do and how I must behave. Yet, amongst this, I find new information, new knowledge, new understanding of others and myself. By looking closely, I can see the similarities between my granddaughter, my daughter, and my wife. I smile gently as I think about it. They are so identical, it is truly amazing. Where yesterday I would look at their interaction and attempt to modify one of them, today I try to smile, as best I can, as I have not achieved my end state yet. The smile that I look for within myself is for both them and me, for who they are, for their complex similarities, and for me and what I can be.

Late one night, my son and his wife called me; Rich was kind of moving in and out of a spiritual state. He told her they would be here tonight. She asked when, and he said when the cicada started to sing. At first, there were questions, since there had been no cicada around that house. But then it happened, initially a few sounds, and then the cicada burst into deafening song. Loudly they sang, and then he arrived. I tried to start a conversation with him, but he said to wait, if I were there, I would have trouble doing anything but listening to their singing. I waited in silence, and then he began to talk. It was a long conversation, over two hours. At first I tried to take notes, to help me recall the true conversation, as I have in the past. However, I soon put the pen down, to listen. The conversation opened with listening. *"Listen,"* he said. *"Hear the song of the cicada. Their music is deafening."* We listened awhile; I could only hear some sounds picked up from his cell phone.

> *He:[6] These are interesting creatures. They do not attack, they do not bite. They have no way to defend themselves. They come en masse, and their song drowns out the sound of everything: the frogs, the birds, the horns of cars, or the sound of car tires on the asphalt. As if to say, hear nothing but us!*

> *The cicadas have no defense. They are only by numbers, and even though there are those that feed upon them with gluttony, they cannot eat them all. They will still be here, to drive the*

---

[6]   I asked him his name, and he playfully told Sumer, "Tell him Larry Logan," a name that Rich often teased Sumer that they would give a daughter if they were so blessed.

sounds from the sky. They do not need to fight back, bite, sting, or fly away. Eat us, kill us, we will still be here, they sing! Such a powerful message in such a simple insect, don't you agree?

Me: I have never looked at it that way.

He: Perspective. You can look at anything and see the good or look and see the bad, it is all perspective.

She: What about the cockroach?
He: Look how they have survived; they have existed for millions of years.

She: I suppose the virtue of the tick would be patience, even though we see them as so disgusting.

He: Yes, they can wait patiently, sitting on a blade of grass for years for something to walk by to which they may attach themselves.

She: They (the cicadas) are really loud, he said they would be loud tonight. Oh my God, they are so loud.

Me: How do we adjust our perspectives?

He: You ask a lot of questions, do you just wish to fill the silence, to hear yourself talk? If you were here, you would find it hard to do anything but listen to them sing. There are two types of questions: 1. What you need to know, and 2. Ones you know the answer to but need to fill the silence. Ultimately it is the questions that bring us here, the first type. You have questions, lots of them. Filter the ones you really want to ask, versus those to fill silence.

I stopped taking notes and focused my energy on his words. I wanted to hear what he said and understand what I heard. The theme was well established at this point, it was about managing perspectives. We spoke of the impact of war. In war, our soldiers kill to keep from being killed. We honor our soldiers for their personal sacrifice and efforts to perform this difficult task, put themselves in harm's way, and protect their peers and us. On the other side of the coin, the fallen soldiers of our enemy are people, too. They are children, sons, and daughters. They are brothers, sisters, perhaps fathers and mothers. For the spiritual side, the victims of war are all the same. There are no bad, there are no good, just people who have completed their work here and have returned home.

I try my hardest to think of the concept of perspectives; this morning many things zoomed through my mind as I proceeded through my daily ritual. I needed to do some things as a part of my fast, I needed to do others as a part of my daily routine. My schedule and Mimi's schedule were not aligning. I anticipated that she would get frustrated and jump out with unfettered emotion. When this occurred, I worked inwardly to adjust my thoughts, my actions. I tried to understand her perspective and what she needed to do. She needed to check her plants, she needed to straighten the bed. In parallel to this, I needed to clean up after our morning walk. I needed to clean the shower and help her straighten the room. Patience was the key to the morning. Anxious moments were replaced with patience and understanding. The potential for harshness was pushed aside, tenderness given in its place. Together, we reflected on the new cucumbers plucked from the garden, the ripening of the plums, and the newness of fresh tomatoes. Breakfast was prepared and eaten, and then I helped her with her socks and new shoes. She does not generally wear shoes in the house, but due to a foot ailment, her doctor recommended she have arch support, hence the need to wear shoes. She did not put them on of her own accord; she awaited my assistance, perhaps wondering in her own mind if I would simply ignore her needs once again.

Today, together, her, the hound, and I rose early and walked our morning path. The air was cool and crisp, the morning calm and quiet. Sometimes when we walk, I call my mother and talk with her a moment, but on this morning, I just needed to enjoy the moment, quietly, without interruption. We walked, the three of us, not talking, just walking quietly. I did not think about the destination or the path that I would take. The path was really understood, we could go this way or that, a turn here and a turn there; sooner or later, we would find ourselves at another junction where we had been many times before on different days. It really did not matter, the purpose was to enjoy the morning, to catch the sun as it rose above the horizon and then watch nature unfold to its radiant beams of light. The birds awake, and then, one of my most favorite morning experiences occurs: huge flocks of birds rise into the sky and take up a path that passes overhead, their wings fluttering rapidly, masked by their morning chirping. As they pass, they begin to scatter, some landing on rooftops, some on the grass. They too follow a morning ritual, unceasingly, each day arising and proceeding down a path of adventure: rise, fly, land, eat, play, fly, eat, and play more, then at the end of the day roost until it is time to rise again. There is no fixed destination, only a daily journey, a journey whose outcome is controlled only by the perspective held within the heart of the traveler.

This morning, I was called upon by my inner self to write these thoughts such that you may feel what I am feeling, to see what I see, to try to understand what I seek to understand. I do not possess knowledge. In fact, the more that I discover, the more I understand the depth of my ignorance. It is somewhat of a dichotomy, as to seek knowledge only seems to make you less knowledgeable. I think about what I would do if I could. It is interesting that I dream of leading people, my mind pushes me ever forward. There I am, a boy, sitting in the pasture, daydreaming of what could be. Every day is a repeat of that moment, the dreams change in scope, not in desire. I look at the world and imagine that I serve it as a leader, perhaps a senator, a president. I have asked about that path, and I am told it is a path not presented to me; I am not a politician. If the desire were deep enough, then I could push myself in that direction. Something warns me to be patient, remember the many junctions of the crossing sidewalks, and just walk, walk quietly, together, enjoy the moment, catch the glory of the early morning sunrise, a new day, a new experience, and new knowledge. What I find in my heart, I can easily find in another's. God loves us, each and every one equally and without condition; should we not try to do the same?

FROM SPIRIT TO FLESH

I awoke, rolled over, and gazed into the darkness. It was cold, so dark and cold. I cried softly. There were others around me, I could hear their breathing, I felt crowded, but so alone. Why alone, what was happening? It seemed as if I were missing something, I thought about it, what was this feeling? The thought faded quickly from my memory, I tossed and turned, then whimpered again. "Richie," I heard the familiar call. "Richie, come here." I crawled from the bed and headed in the direction of the voice. A man was there. "What's the matter, boy?" he asked. He picked me up and placed me between him and the woman. "You hungry?" he asked. He pulled back her gown and said, "See here, here, go ahead and nurse this." I looked at him, I looked at her, and then I climbed over him and down onto the floor. I wandered back into the earlier room, crawled back upon the bed, sat there, and wondered, "Why am I here?"[7]

Why am I here? I have often pondered this piercing question. What is my purpose? Why did God send me here, in this form, this life of suffering and pain? My mind is full of questions and dreams. At an early age, I looked around myself and created my future in my dreams. I was born and raised in the northern Missouri country. In this modest countryside, my parents worked hard to house and feed their four sons. My father, an arrogant yet loving man, was torn between his urge to live the single life of alcohol, women, and pride, and the conflicting role of father and husband. Yes, he was proud to have his four strong and healthy sons. They were his legacy. For my father, life was made up of three principal elements. These elements were composed first of fear.

---

[7] This is an event in my memories, I think I was not older than two, perhaps three.

It was important for everyone to be totally aware of how tough you are and to fear you. This was the absolute top of his list of three. Without that complete dominance of others, the remainder meant very little. He was the alpha male, the ruler of the pack. The second element was sex. He was the alpha male, and therefore he had total choice of all of the females of the pack. The women that he encountered were either his mother, his sister, or available as a sexual partner. The last element was family. He believed that it was important to leave behind a legacy of family that was as powerful as himself.

Father was extremely proud of my oldest brother due to his physical toughness and work drive. He was also proud of his second son, not only for his intelligence, but also for his total lack of fear, his courage, and his ruthlessness. This son was like a bulldog, unafraid and powerful. This son was willing to take the pain in the battle to achieve his locking hold that would ultimately defeat his opponents. His third son was so handsome, tall, slender, the choice of all the girls. My father lived the fantasy of what this boy could accomplish with all the ladies he met. He was unstoppable, yet he was afraid to take advantage of this manly gift. He held tight to a tender and compassionate element that prevented him from going too far, yet these same elements would leave him in torment. He was drawn to religion as a tool to ease his torment. I often think of that torment. He was the third, overshadowed by the power of the two eldest sons. Unable to attain a status of the "big boys,"[8] he was left to survive as one of the "little boys." I would guess that this left him empty, pushing him to try to prove he was greater than a little boy. The family would not permit it. The emptiness would drive him to other family: cousins and aunts. From here he would fall susceptible to the temptations that the negative energies threw at him. His struggle with life continues, but not all negative. He has a complete love of family. He raised first his own daughters, and then his granddaughter, providing her the complete love of family. Yes, her mother loved her, but she was a young mother, and the trials of the time led to one thing and then another; it was just easier for Mom and Dad to raise their grandchild. I don't know all of the details; I just believe that my brother

---

8   Our family would collectively refer to my two older brothers as "the big boys," while the two youngest of the brothers were "the little boys."

was given an opportunity to do it all once more, to gain the additional insight of unconditional love.

I remember the day that my brother was "saved." The reverend was sitting in the dining room, he had been talking about the power of the savior and what was necessary to become saved. My brother held onto every word and then, crying, prayed for forgiveness and followed the Reverend's direction. I must have been about six or seven at the time, and I followed along with my brother. He was doing it, so I guessed I should as well. It was a day or so later that we went to the lake, and the reverend plunged us in the water to cleanse our sins. This latter was an important part of the ritual. After all, how could one expect to ascend to heaven unless they had bathed?

Finally, there was me, the philosopher, negotiator, dreamer, plump and slow, and afraid of everything. I am the youngest of the four; while growing up, I was overshadowed by their presence, watching and waiting. Waiting for something, but not really knowing what. I learned early of the gifts that God has given man. These gifts were outlined in my father's rules, rules that were reinforced in biblical references. To reinforce the rules, my father had a ruler that hung in the kitchen so that each boy could understand where they stood in terms of manliness. Some may think that the ruler was only a joke, something to tease and laugh about. But no, this ruler was etched in my memory; I worried that I could not measure up to the expectations and therefore was not worthy. It was a memory that affected every moment of my life, the self-doubt that occurred for each anticipated relationship with a woman.

I think about the power of my older brothers. Though he denies this, my eldest brother loved to fight and enjoyed inflicting pain. Yes, he also was tormented, but it was hidden well, and his love for hurting was completely evident. He ruled by power; none in the family tree could even begin to challenge that power. I was afraid to fight, logically so, given that all of my battles were with an older brother who simply beat me down. To me, fighting was all about receiving pain, not giving pain. It was something to avoid.

In terms of my personality traits, those were established early in life. I dreamed of being more than I was and attached myself to the surroundings of the time. During this early part of my life, existence was all about the farm, and so I sank my dreams and desires into the thoughts and passion of the farm and its resources. To propagate my dreams, every Christmas everyone knew what I would ask Santa to bring me for a gift. It was the same each and every year that I can remember, up until my seventh Christmas. It was always a farm set that included a metal barn, horses, cows, fences, and tractors. I would set them up and look upon the scene and dream. Then when summer would come, they would find my brother and me outside, behind the house, in the dirt, with fields plowed and planted, neat and orderly. He would generally get impatient and mess up the fields, as the lines had to be perfect. Not me, I would continue to put the rows into the dirt; they did not have to be perfect, they just had to exist.

It was during these years that we moved two times, ending up on an eighty-acre farm there in northern Missouri. I was now past my eighth year, and the farm sets stopped coming. In their place you could still find me sitting outside in a field, daydreaming. I would sit and dream of barns, tractors, horses, and cows. There would be fields planted and always the livestock. Sometimes, there would not be enough room for everything, and I would have to buy up land from the neighbors in order to expand the farm. There on the northeast corner of the farm, a better place for a milk barn. On the northwest corner, beef cattle would graze. And here, next to the house, horses. Beautiful and proud, they would be galloping across the fields. There they were, the sons of the infamous racehorse, Man-of-War, all tall and fast. I read books, Walter Farley's *Black Stallion* series and Laura Wilder's *Little House on the Prairie*. The latter because a school teacher started reading a chapter a day in the afternoon, but I was impatient and needed to get to the end faster than she would allow.

Still, I would dream of what could be, what might exist if I had an opportunity to create it. Strangely, though, I was completely terrified of livestock. This terror had to be suppressed, as it was a weakness and vulnerability that could be manipulated against me by my three older brothers or earn disappointment from my father. No, I had to carry the secret alone; fear, fear of livestock, heights, and water. Then there were things that I could not bring myself to touch: fish, earthworms, crayfish, turtles, and snakes. These were all offensive creatures. Daily farm chores were difficult to accomplish given my fears. The thought of going out and about with the livestock caused internal terror, my stomach would hurt, my chest would be tight. Sometimes, I would try to convince my mother that I was sick, but that could rarely be acknowledged. So I would generally head out to do what I was told. The older brothers took almost the entire load of managing the farm and doing the work. I was little help, and my father was preoccupied with his job and night life. The farm operated because of his commitment to provide direction and guidance to the family legacy. As I grew older, the dreams of the farm turned to thoughts of rebuke; nothing could be further from my mind that continuing a life on a farm. My desire was to escape from that land, to do something more meaningful with my life.

The 1960s were characterized by the nation's race to the moon, but darkened by the escalation of the war in Vietnam and racial conflicts. Every chance I had, I would watch the news to see the coverage of the Apollo space launches. I would hear the talk of the scientist and engineers that made this happen. What could I do to become one of these scientists? Another daydream developed. Another desire was born. Shadowing that desire was worry. Worry about the conflicts that were everywhere. My father ranted about the atrocities being committed by the minorities. He swore allegiance to George Wallace and believed in segregation. He had his reasons; I just did not understand the hatred. My brother fell in love with a young lady visiting in the neighborhood. My father forbid the relationship, she was Catholic. I was young; I did not understand the difference, why did it matter? Another desire was born, the desire to understand.

> *"He who sits on the universal plane breathes the flame of desire into the hearts of man. Those who accept that desire will feel its warmth; those who do not will feel its pain, pain which is the lack of desire."*[9]

---

[9]   From Rich's notes, he first quoted these words to me on the phone.

My desire was real, the desire to know more, to be more, to do something different. I struggled to be a part of something, to be included. The lack of inclusion would at times leave me alone, but it did not really bother me that much. It was just an obstacle to overcome. I looked at where I was. I thought about where I wanted to be. I then devised plans that would get me from where I was to there, the place I wanted to be. These were mental plans, imagination at work. Behind me, unseen but often felt, were those who watch over me, their silent messages entering into my subconscious and helping me with my critical life decisions.

The questions remain: Why am I here? Why are you here? And then, why do many creatures on this earth exist? For this latter question, I have thought a great deal about the butterfly. When I look at this insect and the progression of its existence from birth to death, it is absolutely amazing. So I asked, why did God put this creature here? I think about it a moment. It hatches from its egg and then crawls about in its caterpillar stage, eating and growing and eating more. Then, it weaves a cocoon, where it begins its metamorphosis. From that cocoon rises the butterfly; large colorful wings, fully spread, it flutters among the flowers for all to see its glory; my, what a sight to behold. But what is its purpose, just that we may see its beauty? Perhaps it is no more than that, but I have always tended to think of it as a message for us from God. Think about it for a moment, if he would bring such glory to the butterfly, then what does it mean in terms of the glory he has for us? We, who are created in his image, are blessed with the freedom of choice and are provided many simple messages that reveal the path ahead, should I take the time to listen and observe? When the time comes and we have completed our work here in our human form, then will we also go through a metamorphosis? Will we transition from flesh to spirit, and rise in our beautiful glory, returning back home to God?

I believe the answer is yes and that, to me, is the purpose of the butterfly, to show us what is to come. The butterfly is an example of transition for us. I suppose some would then follow on with this example to say that at our physical death, we transcend into a cocoon like existence and then await the second coming of Christ, where we will then emerge and fly. From new information that I have been given, and my understanding of that information, I think the answer is no, we do not wait for anyone, just ourselves. Our transition begins at birth as we go through the human development process. We are young and grow old. Aging is the constant transformation of our physical being. As this happens, we also go through a spiritual transformation. A lot of this is invisible to our consciousness, and we often receive a plethora of conflicting information. All of this information fills our minds to include questions, thoughts, and answers. We sink down into our physical lives and focus on our glory here on earth. Yes, to be successful at one thing or another is important to most of us. We suffer our pride, our conceit, and our own arrogance. Toward what end, is it only to satisfy the purpose of our existence in this lifetime, to leave a legacy for our heirs, or is it something more significant and eternal than a single lifetime could ever achieve?

THE DREAM

On day, in late February or early March 2006, I arrived at the hospital, where Mimi awaited. She has just undergone a total knee replacement. When I entered her room, she looked at me strangely and then said, "Did you see her? Did you see her?" "See who?" I asked. She looked at me and then said:

> I was lost, I was wandering the hallways, looking for the nurse's station, but could not find it. It began to frustrate me. I went down this hall, then another, but could not find my way. It was then that I heard her:
>
> She asked, "Are you okay?"
>
> I said, "Yes, I am."
>
> She said, "Are you trying to find the nurse's station?"
>
> I said, "Yes, I am, but I don't know where it is."
>
> She reached over and took my hand. "Let me show you."
>
> "You know the way?" I asked.
> As I looked down at a small beautiful child, her long red hair flowing around her head, she said, "Yes, follow me."

We walked down this hall, turned, and walked down another. So gently she led me down the complicated path. Then there, there it was, the nurse's station, I knew where I was; I looked at her, but could not see her face.

I said, "Thank you so much. It was so nice of you to help me find my way back. What is your name?"

She giggled ever so sweetly. "Grandma, I'm Hannah." I gasped, turned my head quickly to see her face, but she was gone.

There was a sound and I awoke, I tried to go back to sleep, to see her face, but it was too late.

Note: Hannah was born to our daughter about four months later. She is a beautiful child with a gentle complexion and red hair. She loves her Grandma dearly.

These feelings, these dreams, what can they be, what do they represent? It is an interesting question; I don't really have the answer. I have thought on it for many years. In 1986, I tried to write a book, *To Be a Man*. I did not have a plan for the book, just another approach to talk about my life, thoughts, and feelings. In this case, I wrote in the introduction:

> *"He is here, I know it, I can feel it, his presence. He is just off the corner, out of my sight, but there in my mind. I try to shrug him away, but he is persistent. Sometimes he takes control; I know when this happens as I have little ability to change what I am doing; it is like I am looking on from the outside. I fear his presence. It is he who writes this book, and it is he who has these thoughts, not I. I think that soon, soon he will take complete control. I think that he will take control when this book is complete. When the book is complete, then I will be no more, and it will be him and him alone."*

That is the basic recollection of what I wrote at that time. I don't know what happened to the pages I wrote; they were on a computer disk. Perhaps if I looked, I would find it somewhere, but it is not important. It was just a step toward understanding.

LEARNING BY REFERENCE

I have wandered around to give you a quick glimpse of things from early childhood to the present. It may seem rambling and appear broken. If we think long and hard on what was said, and we look across our lives, it may be possible to observe that same wandering. Let me organize the flow a little. What I am addressing is the first transition we experience, that transition from our spiritual lives to our human form. This transition is the first part of the angelic transition sequence, 8-2-8. Early in our lives, as infants, we possess more memory of what we were. Those memories fade over time, and in that same time, we begin to add to our memory our current experiences. I will call this latter experience, "learning by reference." What this means to me is that we basically cleanse from our memory cells, in this spirit-to-human metamorphism, all memory of the past. Honestly, I think "cleansing" may be an incorrect way to define it. I could, for example, state that it is always there and that we will come back to it later, in terms of total recollection, but if we just accept that because we cannot use that memory, then it isn't there, and that will suffice for the moment to say it is cleansed.

To continue, I try to understand that we really start with a basic set of default actions, and from there we quickly gather and add into our current memory the experiences and knowledge of this lifetime. When I say learning by reference, what I mean is that we start with little information. We experience warmth, cold, hunger, thirst, love, and pain. Each of these are new feelings from the outside, but deep inside, our soul knows and understands them. Also, gathered around us every moment are our spirit guides, guardian angels, and other messengers of God. They are constantly giving us the information we need to grow. We ultimately will call this set of directions our inner voice, our unconscious thoughts, our sixth sense. All of this interaction is very important in the early years. It will help us adjust to our new surrounding as our memory of home slowly fades.

Moving through time, we encounter new experiences. We ask questions, gather information about the experience, comparing the experience with something else we have in our memory. A new memory is added. This experience is like something that we already know, except it is different in this way. For example, consider hate. We don't start with knowledge of hate; we only understand love and tenderness. When we encounter hate, we think, what is it? We search our memory to find something similar. It feels like an emotion, but empty, cold, and without God. We could compare it to love. Love is fullness, warmth, with God. Perhaps then hate is the opposite of love, or the absence of love. If God is love, and hate is the absence of love, then hate is the absence of God. Look, now we have added something to our reference database. Within our early memory, we had stored our understanding of love. Love is defined as warm, tender, and of God. We then used learning by reference to add a new experience to our memory. That memory is about hate, cold, harsh, and without God.

We learn by reference. We limit our understanding to what we know. Unfortunately, that restricts our spiritual development. It restricts us in that we must understand fully what we do not know. He that came before spoke of this, you will find it referenced in Christian religious books. He stated that those around him could not understand what he said of the world and people, of things they could see and hear. So for him to speak of God and spiritual ways, he put the burden on everyone to accept and understand what they could not see and hear. When he spoke about home and stated that only those who came from there would return there, it was confusing and suggested a limitation on our ability to return home. The fact, as I understand it, was that he was confirming that we all, being born of the essence of God, would return to God, each and every one, according to our desire. This is an important confirmation for me, to understand the words written in history and spoken to me. The message is clear, we are all created in the essence of God and have all come from home, by our own choice to live a life in human form, and that when the time comes we will return home. 8-2-8, the angelic transition sequence, starts with the transition from the spiritual form to the human form. I quote from Zophiel again:

He: The Powerball sequence 8 – 2 – 8, death and birth, flesh and spirit, birth and death, it is an angelic sequence, it is a metamorphosis, like the caterpillar to a butterfly, the maggot to a fly. It is a transition. We all experience transitions. Do you understand?

Me: I think I do.

He: Don't think, thinking is superficial, only skin deep, on the surface, it does not reach to the soul. Accept. 828, the Powerball sequence, it is about transitions. You and Mimi make your own transitions. Transitions occur; they only occur if you want them to.

I have read about the coming and going that we experience in various writings of well-known psychic and spiritual books. Their stories are consistent with information that I have received, though each is periled by issues of interpretation. From this I understand that we come and we go. No, it is not reincarnation to which I refer, it is spiritual metamorphism. From home we devise a plan for our earthly visit. We gather our support team and together devise a plan for a life in human form. Generally, there is a task that we want to perform, an imperfection that we want to fix. Perhaps we devise a plan to correct an imperfection from a previous human form, perhaps something else. But ultimately it is our soul plan. The plan is for the development of our soul, our spiritual self. That plan is filed and available for review later, when we return home. There are some on earth that are given psychic vision; it is a part of their plan. These few are able to read the plans of others (but never their own).

UNDERSTANDING TIME AS A FUNCTION OF REALITY

In human form, our lives are defined in terms of time. We are born at hour one, and at some hour x, we will pass from this life. That interval could be hours, days, months, or years. Nominally, I believe the average life span is in excess of seventy years. It really doesn't matter how long, from a spiritual perspective, only that in the human form, our lives are a function of time. What we live, our human existence, becomes our reality. As stated earlier, our memories of home quickly fade, and we are left with what we learn in this new life. Our reality is what we live in the present form, and in that present form, we exist as a function of time. We could then express this in the term where we, in human form, are a function of time, and that reality is a function of our human form, therefore time must equal reality, or expressed differently, time and reality are each a function of the other. I will simplify this expression as reality is a function of time or life = f(reality/time) where time (t) approaches X (t » X) such that the maximum value of X is the life span of man in years for a single metamorphism.

I understand that God has always existed. God is and always will be. In addition, I can say that time, as we know and understand it, does not exist in the spiritual universe. Forty minutes or forty million years is just the same. Some have said that our average life span of seventy years could be equated to five minutes in the spiritual universe, but that would mean that time exists, only at a different rate. If that were true, then life on the other side would be a function of time, and then God would exist as a function of time and ultimately be susceptible to old age and death. This thought does not make sense; God is and always will be, which simply means that time does not exist in that domain. If time does not exist, and our reality is a function of time, then our reality does not exist or is undefined within that universe (example: our life = f(reality/time, where time = 0 is undefined mathematically). But we do exist, so it may be that our life in human existence is only an illusion in the spiritual world.

15 Oct 2010 Notes of the evening

We retired to the back porch and sat there around the table, playing rummy. At 7:30 p.m. he got up and returned with a scotch, for himself and me, and a cigar, as it was time for my 200 calorie meal. We drank the scotch and played cards with his mother and wife. This went on until about 10 p.m., when the game finally concluded. During the evening I kept hearing the house blinds bump the window frame but there was little wind that could cause this effect. I would look around, I knew we were not alone, but I do not have vision to see. The conversations turned to snacks, and he said that he enjoyed chocolate cookie dough. He said that they had some in the refrigerator, and I suggested a chocolate chip pop tart. As I got up he told me not to get anything, as if he really wanted the cookie dough, he would just change the cigar. I chuckled to myself and went to the pantry and retrieved a package of pop tarts. I sat them on the table in front of him and returned to my chair at the end of the table. He was sitting there in a hooded sweatshirt; he shivered a couple of times. He looked very relaxed, almost ready to fall to sleep; he would take a pull on the cigar and then be silent for a few moments. When he shivered again his wife wrapped him in a blanket as the temperature had now dropped below 68 degrees. He then reached over for the cigar and bit off an end. He smiled his sheepish grin and said, "Now that is good," as he chewed on the cigar. His wife looked closely at him and said, "What are you doing? That will make you sick," and then reached over for the cigar butt that he had returned to the ash tray. She picked it up, smelled it, and then took a nibble. She looked at me and exclaimed, "This is chocolate!" She handed it to me, and sure enough, it was a chuck of chocolate cookie dough. I toyed with it a moment, and a piece broke off and fell on the floor. I handed one part back to her then picked up the piece on the floor and placed it on the table. I pointed out to Mimi what was happening, and she picked up the piece of chocolate, smelled it, and then took a taste. She admitted that it was indeed chocolate cookie dough. I noticed that the two pieces of chocolate had joined together into one piece once again. We sat there talking and watching him for the next half hour, and then he said we should go inside. I got up and started cleaning the table, picking up the cups and glasses. As I went to dump the ashtray he reached over and picked up the remains of the cookie dough. After I had dumped the ashtray and put it back on the table he laid the cookie dough back in the tray and said that he would probably finish smoking it come morning. We went inside, all admitted they were tired, and we all retired for the night.

At 9 a.m. the following morning, I went to the porch and in the ashtray was the remains of the cigar butt from the night before. At 11 a.m. he went out, picked up the butt, and finished smoking it.

So, my repeated question is, why have I gone through this discussion? First I wanted to give an example of what we collectively observed over one evening's time. An object existed, in this case a cigar; it changed to something else, as witnessed by the three of us, and then returned to its original structure by the following morning. What really occurred physically cannot be explained by me, I only witnessed it. From a physical perspective, I could just call it an illusion. From the spiritual perspective, I could admit that anything is possible at any time, that even our existence could be only an illusion. From what I understand, we exist here for only a brief moment in terms of our spiritual existence. During this period of human existence, the most important thing that we do is protect our soul. We are vulnerable in human form. We protect ourselves within our plan by choosing spirit guides and guardian angels to help us during this time that we allow ourselves to be vulnerable. God provides angels to help us and deliver us messages. These messages, subliminal thoughts, communications in dreams, heartfelt emotions, are all provided to help us reach the goals of our plan. But whether we follow the plan or not is our choice, for God has given us free will. He gives us total free will, freedom of choice, to do whatever we choose. That is what God has given to us. For all of that, he asks of us nothing. He does not judge, he does not hate, he does not condemn, he does not destroy. God gives us everything. He gives us his love. He gives us unhindered, unconditional, total, and complete love. Infinite love that is eternal.

THE DEFINITION OF LOVE

Let me take a brief aside and talk about love. Do you know love? I mean, can you define it, use it in a sentence? Do you feel it, receive it, use it? Consider the following:[10]

> *Love is an emotion.*
>
> *Love is pain.*
>
> *Love is possessing.*
>
> *Love is a feeling.*

---

[10] Rich presented this discussion to me on the phone one evening. It was not clear to me his exact state at the time, but it was a very inspiring for me. I did not capture the exact transcript but tried to summarize it from my memory.

Love is caring.

Love is giving.

Now, a sentence:

I love my car.

I love my home.

I would love to go with you.

I just love to eat.

I love to walk.

I love you.

I love it.

I would love to.

Let's make love!

Well, it seems like there are a lot of uses for the word. If I consider each use, I can find some similar uses; for example, I love my car and I love my home seem similar: owning something. I love to walk and I love to eat may be similar: enjoying something. Basically this just means that the word is overused, its meaning has digressed to something less important. So, in essence, you hear or read, "God loves you." You think, "That is nice, I love him too." Or you think, "Yeah, so why doesn't he give me a new car, if he loves me so much?" Or, "If he really loves me, then why did this or that happen?" The typical response is to bring the context of God's love into our understanding and normal everyday use of the word "love," and that is not what we are being given, that general everyday use of the word.

How can I explain my understanding of the phrase, "God loves you"? I could try to use some adjectives such as total, complete, enduring, unconditional, eternal, pure, simple, unending, extraordinary, deep, wide, expansive, infinite, or fully. I could say that to have a complete and total understanding of his love would mean that you would die, as you could not exist without being closer to it, and the closest way is to be at home, where you feel his love completely. Though we often attempt to describe love, or bound it in terms like as "high as the mountains, or deep as the sea," the fact is that God's love is not something you can put into a container or limit by superficial thoughts and expectations. It has been explained to me that God's love is so absolutely unconditional that even the worst villain of your nightmares is loved unconditionally by him. Yes, Hitler, Saddam Hussein, the rapist, the pedophile, Satan, they are all loved equally by him. "He loves all of his children, even the ones that make him cry." The following scenario was presented:

> *He:[11] A person came into your house and destroyed everyone there, all of your family, young and old, tortured you, burned your house, took everything you ever had, ever wanted. Then you stand before this person and reach out your arms, pulling them close, and say, God loves you and therefore I love you and forgive you.*

It is completely foreign to our human thought and capability. If you could understand how to do this, you would be given a glimpse of his love. His love is that deep, and because of the depth of his love, we are given freedom, freedom to choose, choice without conditions or constraints. There is only one rule: God loves us, and when we are ready to return home, he will receive us with open arms, unconditionally. The choice of accepting his love is our own. What restricts us is what we do, and how we do it. If we could truly understand that level of love, we would be able to show that same love to others. Thus the thought of taking atrocious actions against others would be eliminated, as the desire to do anything other than love would be eliminated. If you look closely at the words in the Book of Robes, you will read where David presented this same argument.

As referenced in the NIV Psalm 6:8–10:

> *Away from me, all you who do evil, for the Lord has heard my weeping. The Lord has heard my cry for mercy; the Lord accepts*

---

[11] This dialog comes directly from Rich. I do not think he was "in spirit" at the time, he was just teaching me.

my prayer. All my enemies will be ashamed and dismayed; they will turn back in sudden disgrace.

As referenced in the NIV Psalm 36:5–9:

Your love, O Lord, reaches to the heavens, your faithfulness to the skies. Your righteousness is like the mighty mountains, your justice like the great deep. O Lord, you preserve both man and beast. How priceless is your unfailing love! Both high and low among men find refuge in the shadow of your wings. They feast on the abundance of your house; you give them drink from our river of delights. For with you is the fountain of life; in your light we see light.

We choose to write a plan, to implement that plan, and come to this existence. But we do not retain the conscious memory of that plan. To do so would impair the freedom of choice. If we knew the plan, then it would be a concrete direction for us to follow. We would be slaves to the plan and thus have no free will. So, as I stated earlier, because God has given us freedom of choice, free will, the full knowledge of our plan must be hidden from us. What is left are memories and heart-felt emotions, memories and emotions that can be assisted from God's messengers, our spirit guides and guardian angels. To hear those messages, we must choose to do so. But choosing to do so comes with its own perils, as once we open the door, then we open ourselves to not only the messages from God, but also false messages. Later in this book, I will discuss how to know the difference, so be careful that you do not just stop here and run off to practice what I have discussed so far. Spiritualism is more than a few words on a piece of paper, and it is difficult to develop without assistance.

As described earlier, on December 6, 2008, I scheduled a discussion with my spiritual advisor. We spoke about my son, and in reference to him, she stated, "Give his life to the light side—to service. Recognize who he is, why are they giving this to him?" This was the gift to me of knowledge of the upcoming events, events that I would be pressed to recognize and accept without her continued guidance and the evolution of his spiritual self, merged with my inclusion within the process.

CHALLENGES OF THE FLESH

I cannot recall the moment of life that it occurred, perhaps in Sunday school, perhaps while listening to conversations of adults. But it did occur, and what it was, was the thought that if you believed hard enough, anything was possible when it came to God. All that was needed was full and complete belief. But inasmuch as that thought seemed so clear to me, I doubted that I could ever achieve that level of belief.

I was just a child of ten years, when on the farm, a new calf was born, like so many that preceded it, and others that followed. This one was different; it was different because of my desire to have something of my own. I had talked to my father about this, but he simply dismissed it. At that same time, I came down with appendicitis, and the night before surgery, my father spoke to me, saying that if I were brave, then the new calf would be mine. This was perhaps one of the first challenges presented to me, a challenge to overcome my fears and find my courage to accept what was about to happen, and remain calm and deliberate despite my deep anxiety. I spent the night worrying, alone in the hospital. Early in the morning, when they wheeled me into the operating room, I was nervous and scared, but I helped them position me on the operating table. As they put the mask to my face, I thought of that calf and focused on my challenges. They applied the ether, I drifted off. When I awoke, I was somewhat disoriented and called out, "I want my ____," thinking mother, but then stopped, remembering the calf. Instead, I corrected myself and, trying to be brave, said, "I want to go to my room."

I returned home from the hospital and took possession of the calf, if not by my father's will, then by my own. I spent the next couple of years there on the home farm, still afraid of all livestock except my own cow, with whom I spent many hours. On or about my twelfth birthday, I found my young cow fallen in a mud bog. I don't know how long she had been there, but she lay there in the mud, tired, eyes glazed. I went to my brothers and asked for help. They, not I, waded into the mud and pushed and pulled and dug and pulled again. Finally, they put a rope around her horns and, with the horse, pulled her from the mud, up onto the bank. The job complete, they suggested I give her grain and water, and they left. I tended to her daily but saw no progress; I worried as I saw her grow weaker with each passing day and begged my father to end her life. One day, I walked up the hill after sitting with her for a while and looked to heaven. I sang a song, and I prayed. I apologized for my failings and tried to believe, to believe hard enough that a miracle could happen. The miracle I sought did not occur, she did not stand.

The next day, my third brother took the tractor, with a lift, down into the ditch, loaded the cow, and hauled her to the garage. We prepare a nice bed for her and gave her water and grain. The next morning she had passed. It was over for the cow, not for me. I worried that I did not believe hard enough.

THE STORY OF TWO ANGELS

How hard it was, to live on this farm, afraid of the livestock, but more afraid that others would know of my fear. I will talk more about fear later, but what is important here is the understanding of belief and miracles. I think of a story, a simple story, a parable.[12] If you could give me license for creativity and let me tell you the story as it was told to me, then with your permission I will do so.

> *There met in heaven two angels, one with more experience and knowledge of earth and man, who we will call the old angel,*

---

[12] This is another of the many stories told to me by Rich. In this case I do not think he was "in spirit." Instead, he was in a teaching mood, trying to help me understand angelic gifts.

and the other of no experience of earth and man, who we will call the young angel.

The two angels were talking, and the young asked the old about the earth. What is it like there, he asked. The other said, very interesting but things are not always what they seem. The young angel asked that he be shown earth, and the older one agreed. They appeared on the earth, worn and tattered, dressed as two beggars walking the road. They walked most of the day, looking at all the earth could offer their vision at one time, hearing the sounds of life, feeling the sun, shade, and soon the cold chill of night. When nightfall came upon them they approached a huge home. They knocked at the door, and when a man appeared the older of the two said, "We are but two tired and weary travelers, we have nothing to offer but only ask for a place to sleep for the night and if there be something available to eat, we are very hungry."

The man looked at them with disgust, but taking pity on them, he stated that he had room in the basement where they could sleep. He led them there and stated he would be back shortly. In an hour or so he returned with food scraps left over from his dinner that he gave the travelers and then tossed them a couple of horse blankets. "You may sleep on the floor, this will keep you warm; at first light you must be gone," he stated. With that he left. They ate the scraps and then lay down to sleep under the blankets. In the early morning, just as the sun was rising, the young angel awoke to see the older angel working on the wall. With calm professionalism the old angel repaired crack after crack in the old foundation of the building. When he completed his task he turned to the young angel and said it was time to leave. The angels continued their journey. An hour or so later the man of the home entered his basement, saw the two beggars had left, and then saw the repairs on his wall. He smiled and said, "Look here, I took in two beggars from the road, fed them, and gave them a place to sleep and God has rewarded me with this blessing, that they would repay my kindness by fixing my basement walls. How blessed I am," he exclaimed as he went back up the stairs to eat his breakfast.

As the angels walked on, they gazed at all of nature and rejoiced in all of its presence; the young angel was so amazed by all that he saw, yet he was slightly confused about the basement. Still, he did not say anything, but as night grew close he asked his companion what they would do this night. The old angel smiled and said, "Just up here, you will see," and then around the bend there appeared a small humble cottage. They approached the door and an old man appeared. Once again the angel introduced themselves and the man quickly ushered them into the house where he presented their story to his wife. His wife quickly pulled up a couple of rocking chairs close to the fireplace and sat the two travelers, and then she brought a couple of blankets from her bed to cover them. She said they must be cold from the night chill and then rushed away to return with warm cider. "Drink this," she said, "it will warm you." She then scurried off to return a few minutes later with a loaf of fresh bread and homemade cheese, slices of roast chicken, and a jar of peach preserves. She begged them to eat, they must be hungry. The old angel asked the man and his wife to join them, but they insisted that they had already eaten, but to please eat their fill. As the evening progressed the old couple brought more pillows and blankets and after ensuring their guests were comfortable and warm they retired for the night.

Come daybreak the young angel awoke to see the old angel looking out the window at the old couple now standing in their pasture, staring down at a dead milk cow, the lady crying; what would they do now with their only cow dead? The young angel said, "What has happened here?" The old angel said, "Do not lose heart, things are not as they seem." To which the young angel replied, "Why was this allowed to happen? Yesterday we stayed in a home where the man treated us so terribly, putting us in a damp basement with nothing but horse blankets to keep us warm, feeding us his scraps, and for that you repaired the walls of his home. Now, this old couple have given us everything, even the food they were about to eat, going hungry themselves and you allow their cow to die."

The old angel looked at the other and said, "Things are not always as they seem. In the other house, when I woke, there were sun rays entering into the basement, and I saw a glint behind the walls. Looking closely I saw that there was a large gold vein behind the walls and quickly patched the wall so that the man would not find it. As to this couple, last night the Angel of Death came to take the farmer's wife, and I said to him, "If you must take something, take the cow instead."

This is such a simple story, so simple yet difficult to understand. It is just not the case to think that God rewards us with riches, or that because we have property or wealth, we are blessed by God, or that God does not loves us if we are poor. God loves us, each and every one. So, if God loves us, why is this necessary? If we totally understood the question, then perhaps we could better understand the answer. I suppose that we pretend to understand, while we struggle to learn, to gain knowledge, and to gain understanding. I ask of them, who would speak with me about why the suffering is necessary? The answer: you cannot know the "with" unless you have experienced the "without." We're born into a life of suffering, we are human, and we have left the protection of the other side to come into this life. We have left home, where pain does not exist and there is only love, to come here in human form and to experience, to work on our perceived faults. We're not sent here, we choose to come. The choice is ours, our desires, part of free will. Free will is a gift of God. The pain and suffering is by our own creation. It is not from them. They do not control, they do not direct; they are just supportive of our own plans and desires. They do not provide mitigation; they only provide us support and encouragement to endure.

THE SEVEN DEADLY SINS

The challenges of the flesh that we must face each and every day can be summed up in the seven deadly sins or cardinal sins. These are described in various ways, but for the most part consist of the following (a search of the Internet will reveal multiple descriptions, this is a summary of one such search):

Lust: excessive thoughts or desires of a sexual nature.

Gluttony: the overindulgence and overconsumption of anything to the point of waste.

Greed: very excessive or rapacious desire and pursuit of wealth, status, and power.

Sloth: the failure to utilize one's talents and gifts, laziness and indifference.

Wrath: anger, or rage, an inordinate and uncontrolled feeling of hatred and anger. These feelings can manifest as vehement denial of the truth, both to others and in the form of self-denial, impatience, and generally wishing to do evil or harm to others.

Envy: an insatiable desire or resentment of another person that has something perceived as lacking in themselves and wishing the other to be deprived of it.

Pride: considered the original and most serious of the seven deadly sins, and indeed the ultimate source from which the others arise. It is a desire to be more important or attractive than others. Failing to acknowledge the good work of others, and excessive love of self (especially holding one's self out of proper position toward God).

In addition to these, recognized within the Roman Catholic Church are seven virtues. These are chastity, temperance, charity, diligence, patience, kindness, and humility.

THE SEVEN VIRTUES

The description of these virtues may be found on the Internet at en.wikipedia.org/wiki/Seven_virtues. This site offers the following descriptions:

Chastity: abstaining from sexual conduct according to one's state in life; the practice of courtly love and romantic friendship. Cleanliness through cultivated good health and hygiene, and maintained by refraining from intoxicants. To be honest with one's self, one's family, one's friends, and all of humanity. Embracing of moral wholesomeness and achieving purity of thought, through education and betterment. The ability to refrain from being distracted and influenced by hostility, temptation, or corruption.

Temperance: restraint, temperance, justice. Constant mindfulness of others and one's surroundings; practicing self-control, abstention, moderation, zero-sum, and deferred gratification. Prudence to judge between actions with regard to appropriate actions at a given time. Proper moderation between self-interest and public interest, and against the rights and needs of others.

Charity: Generosity, charity, self-sacrifice; the term should not be confused with the more restricted modern use of the word charity to mean benevolent giving. In Christian theology, charity—or love (agapé)—is the greatest of the three theological virtues. Love, in the sense of an unlimited loving kindness toward all others, is held to be the ultimate perfection of the human spirit, because it is said to both glorify and reflect the nature of God. In its most extreme form, such love can be self-sacrificial. Confusion can arise from the multiple meanings of the English word "love." The love that is "caritas" is distinguished by its origin—being divinely infused into the soul—and by its residing in the will rather than emotions, regardless of what emotions it stirs up. This love is necessary for salvation, and with it no one can be lost.

Diligence: a zealous and careful nature in one's actions and work, decisive work ethic, steadfastness in belief, fortitude, and the capability of not giving up. Budgeting one's time; monitoring one's own activities to guard against laziness. Upholding one's convictions at all times, especially when no one else is watching (integrity).

Patience: forbearance and endurance through moderation. Resolving conflicts and injustice peacefully, as opposed to resorting to violence. The ability to forgive, to show mercy to sinners. Not killing or being violent in any way to any life form or sentient being; to practice moderation of meat consumption and consistent life ethic. Creating a sense of peaceful stability and community, rather than engendering suffering, hostility, and antagonism.

Kindness: charity, compassion, and friendship for its own sake. Empathy and trust without prejudice or resentment. Unconditional love and voluntary kindness without bias or spite. Having positive outlooks and cheerful demeanor; to inspire kindness in others.

Humility: modest behavior, selflessness, and the giving of respect. Humility is not thinking less of yourself, it's thinking of yourself less. It's a spirit of self-examination; a hermeneutic of suspicion toward yourself and charity toward people you disagree with. The courage of the heart necessary to undertake tasks that are difficult, tedious, or unglamorous, and to graciously accept the sacrifices involved. Reverence for those who have wisdom and those who selflessly teach in love. Giving credit where credit is due; not unfairly glorifying one's own self. Being faithful to promises, no matter how big or small they may be. Refraining from despair, and the ability to confront fear, uncertainty, or intimidation.

I look at myself from the time of my early memories until today and see without doubt that I have been the instrument of each of the sins and have lacked in the practice of the virtues. Today I read over each of these seven virtues and discover the peace of thought that is derived from the words presented. In the past, I would have mocked these words, now I look to find how I may achieve a life that is filled with their practice.

THE TEMPTATIONS OF YOUTH

I was young, I was ignorant. I looked to my role models and tried to find a way to learn from them. The negative energies had their way with me. I fell deeply into lustful desire. I say deeply, as this pain of my life was there from early childhood. Yes, I could claim this was the result of mental abuse, brainwashing that occurred over the years. The question was, what must you do to be a man? The answer varied, but generally it was about sexual conquest. Sexual conquest could only be achieved by the measurement of your manhood. A young mind raced to find information, to learn from others, to see that which was forbidden to young eyes.

The young gathered in the darkness and played games; games that were hidden from adults. I don't know how far it could have gone, without the nagging of what was right and wrong in my mind. But fall, yes I fell far and hung onto the temptations as if they were my only lifelines. I began to question the value of religion and question the teachings of the Bible. Church was not for me, and I justified my decisions based on statements where I simply blamed the hypocritical nature of the people who would go there. I taunted those who prayed for help, who listened to Christian music, and who preached the word according to the Bible. I was young, and I took up vices of drinking alcohol, smoking, profanity, and practicing lust. Each day I would look at myself and ask what it was that I did wrong that I would end up in this body, in this life, while trying harder to add more conquests to my résumé.

Notice, I did not challenge the existence of God, nor did I challenge the existence of evil. What I did was blame my imperfections on everything, including God. I was not worthy of anyone or anything. I doubted myself in all ways. I had all kinds of thoughts in my mind. Dreams, imagination, desires; I worried about these thoughts for years. How would I overcome these nagging thoughts? The answer was not coming directly, it was hidden from view. I did not have time to give to God. I only had time for myself. As time progressed, I would be able to justify each thing I did based on a new rule set. This rule set was simple. Whatever I did was for others and not for me. It was the self-sacrifice for family. Yet, every conversation was about what I had done that day. Look at me, all that I have done for you; when I think of it now, I can hardly write these words. It is painful to fully realize the level to which I fell during this challenging period of my life. To overcome the challenges of the flesh would take more energy than I could possibly derive in my lifetime.

It is at these lowest of our boundaries that the options to reject the existence of God are presented. At these moments, the question that challenged my mind was simple: "Why God would let all of this happen to me? Why would God create this body, this mind?" It doesn't make sense; there must be something else that I am missing. I thought this through so carefully. First, I must accept the fact that God is, there is no other option. Yet general acceptance without something to substantiate that acceptance seems trite. So I look first at myself. I exist. You exist, the earth exists. Animals exist. The universe exists. Next, I think of a writer of songs, books, or editorials, or a painter of art or just general painting. When I think of these people, I find that they have a pattern in their work. You can generally look at the work and discern its creator if you look or listen closely. Their creative thoughts are consistently applied. Given this fact, I look at our world and the universe of what

I can see. Here the patterns are very similar. The structure of animals, sea creatures, birds and fowl, the similarities of a plant's reproductive cycle as compared to animal, and the reproductive cycle of stars. Aging and dying were considered, and after all of this, there could be only one conclusion, it was all created by a single architect, the patterns are applied consistently.

The discussion here was somewhat abbreviated to simplify the point I am trying to make, simplification of something so complex may not be appropriate but I am limited by my own reference database. The point is that the existence of God is accepted by me as truth.

The next question is about God. Is God good? This is a much more complicated question and cannot be adequately explained in a single paragraph. Once again, for simplification, let me think of what a builder or artist creates. Why does the artist create something? Is it because they detest what they create, or do they create what they love? I suppose you could argue that some artists create things of pain, and therefore they create what they hate, but I would argue that they only create what they love, and if they create something of pain, then pain is what they love, and this may be the case as it is what they know (refer back to learning by reference). That is an assertion; I understand that you may not agree. But if an artist creates what they love, then we can say that is good, and therefore we could conclude that God creates only what he loves. So, if he creates what he loves and loves what he creates, then God must be good. It would only make sense. We look at things and see that he created the birds and the fishes, and then we observe the birds eating birds and the fishes eating fishes and so on, and then we say that amongst all of this that God created pain and suffering, so where is the good in this? So, at that point in my life I left the question unanswered.

Biblical passages would suggest that God is capable of wrath and jealousy, both deadly sins. There is clearly some inconsistency of information being presented, but I resolve myself to accept that God does indeed exist, there is no other option. If God exists, then angels exist, and if angels exist, then demons exist, and if demons exist, then they are led by something, and therefore the conclusion is that Satan exists. If both

God and Satan exist, and if one is doing one thing and the other is not, then they are on opposite poles. If they are opposites and God is good, then Satan must be bad. If the angels love God and help him, then they are good, and if demons help Satan, then they are bad. A relationship is formed in my mind. I understand there are roles for both good and bad and that one is the opposite of the other. If angels love God, and they do God's work, and if negative energies (what we call demons) are opposite of God and do Satan's work, then demons must despise God and therefore hinder His work.

(Side note: It is not clear to me that the angels that left God's side and began negative work really despise him, it could be that they love him but despise his creation; man. It could be something else, I will address this later.)

Finally, if good is positive, then the influence of angels is positive, and the opposite of positive forces are negative forces, which then yields that good is positive and bad is negative. In the physical world, we know that magnetic forces exist that are both positive and negative, and that in the magnetic realm, opposites attract and therefore complement each other in our existence. I must be careful and not jump to a conclusion, but I have convinced myself that in order for each of these spiritual elements to exist, that one must be the opposite of the other, therefore one is positive (good) and one is negative (not good), that God created us, in his essence, and that was a positive thing, so then God by inference is good. Enough said at this point to accept this fact, God exists and God is good.

If God created all, then he created the angels and thus created Satan, who was an angel, as well as all of the angels that followed him. This could then be interpreted that negative energy was created by God as well as positive. This argument seems to be another of the dichotomies of the universe. Once again, for simplification, God has given us free will. Free will cannot exist unless there are choices to be made, the choice of one path or another. My conclusion is that good and evil are both divine gifts. It is what we do with those gifts that make the difference for both our physical and spiritual existence.

In summary, for me, God exists and God is good. I understand that the opposite of good exists, call it evil, and that evil exists in order for us, as humans, to have free will. Without free will we would be nothing more than robots or slaves, and where would be the happiness in that? I then conclude that though evil exists, the exact definition of it must be understood before assertions can be made on its benefit.

We could say that Judas was evil because he was a traitor to Jesus. Yet, he loved Jesus and he kissed him because he loved him, whilst doing what he had to do to complete the plan that Jesus had written for himself. To see the good in the actions of Judas is difficult, but that understanding of why he did what he did is really a small picture of the complexities of the universe.

I am trying to see the good in all that happens. It is a difficult challenge, because of the complex interactions that occur on a constant basis. No, I cannot endorse all things that happen as for the best; I cannot say that the assassin's bullet is justified. What I can say is that I do not understand it all, and for that reason I am trying to defer to those who do understand, the burden of judgment.

With this conclusion, I then look at the pain and suffering that plague me and determine that in the past, I believed that the fact that the pain existed must be a part of my own failings. I failed because I did not believe enough. After all, it is in the Book of Robes that Christ said, "Ye of so little faith, why are you afraid?" The answer for me, at that time: I am afraid because I have so little faith, and because I have so little faith, God has not recognized me. It must be true, as I look at the book and find over and over again that those who have faith are rewarded by God and those of power and wealth have achieved this standing because they were in good standing with God. Please understand that this was my thought then, because I understood less then than now.

Next, I think about envy. My early years were filled with envy of what others had that I had not. I did not respect myself, and I did not respect others. I dropped off into a cauldron of envy and distrust. Everyone had something that I did not have. They had physical attractiveness, intelligence, money, girls, cars, friends. They had freedom, and they never appeared to be afraid. I worried about everything, and I was afraid. I was so afraid, but my biggest fear was that someone would find out that I was afraid. Once again my thoughts turned to the pain of my life. I was not born into wealth. I criticized my very existence, my looks, my thoughts, my social skills (or lack thereof). Why would God put me here on this earth, in this form? What did I do wrong? What disease did I have that deformed my physical being? I sought answers to these questions, there must be an answer somewhere. Yet, I sought the answers silently.

I desired friends, but I was not worthy of their friendship, and I could not give to them the same things they shared with each other. My ability to be a friend was blocked by my worry they would discover my deepest secrets and fears. I envied my brothers, their girlfriends. I had the desire to develop relationships, even at a very young age. It was not going to happen because I only wanted the most beautiful and popular of the girls that surrounded me. I would have fantasies of being loved, it left me empty. I started to stare. This was such a tormenting habit. I would stare at girls and boys alike; the girls to fulfill sexual lust; the boys to determine if my imperfections were visible in them, such that I would know if they were visible in me.

As a young adult, in my teens, I began to worry about my fears. At this point in my life, I thought it was necessary to conquer these fears, and I started working on pride. I focused on the development of pride within myself. This pride was born and developed as a pure negative energy. It was not with others, it was in conflict with others. I would become arrogant in the knowledge that I would develop. Look at this combination, pride and arrogance. I must always prove that I knew more about a subject than others. This came at a huge cost. The cost to others. As stated earlier, I did not respect others. I thought that I did at the time, but looking back I see the many things that I did wrong and how it affected others. I did not want to live in the cave any longer. I wanted to climb out into the light with Socrates. To make that climb I had to reach out and grab onto others that could help pull me up the long trail. My mentors were arrogant and prideful, and I skillfully picked up these capabilities and wielded my sword without hesitation.

They carried the attributes that I understood from early childhood were essential elements toward full manhood.

In this social environment, the role of the female was to serve the needs of the male. Women existed to serve man. Short and concise, all I need to do was review in the Book of Robes this documented fact. There in Genesis, woman was made from man's rib, because man was lonely and asked for something. The something given was woman, and it was because of woman that man fell from grace, and therefore her penance was to be the servant of man. How convenient for a man, to have this written into the book and taught every day for thousands of years.

So, I grab onto this excuse for how I conducted my life, roll the wall paper out, spread out the paste on its back, and hang it on the wall until I have covered all of the blemishes that exist. If I can cover it up, if it is not visible, then it won't exist at all. Let it just fester under the paper, that will be okay. I can have my nightmares, hang my head, and blame everything but myself on the trials of life. After all, it is all about the level of society to which you are born. Look at me, poor white country boy, afraid and alone, covered with wall paper.

WALL PAPER[13]

I must digress a moment and discuss the concept of wall paper. Over the past few weeks, I have attempted to do so with a few people; in some cases it appears that I succeeded, in others, I was not so successful. But I must give you a couple of new tools to use, and this anecdote is one such tool.

To begin you must recall, or just imagine, yourself standing within a room, a room for which you claim some form of responsibility, such as in your home or your office. The next step is to look around the

---

[13]   Wall paper is another of the lessons from Rich. Early in 2009 he introduced this concept to me. The concept of removing the wall paper and cleaning the wounds was reinforced in other conversations with him "in spirit" state two.

room and observe its defects. There on the wall across from the door a scratch, or the blemish on the window sill, the nail holes from past curtain or picture hangers. Perhaps the wall's paint has faded from the sun. Perhaps it is old, tattered, and torn. Fragments of time are revealed around the wall, frayed edges, discoloration, and deterioration. You look upon these blemishes and think about how they will look to others that come into the room and, when seeing the defects, what they will think of you and of your home or your office. The quality of their judgment weighs upon your mind. It could be that it is not only discomforting for you in terms of someone else's judgment, but maybe even your own judgment. The room is not comfortable to you. You struggle with the view, you decide something must be done.

The choices are presented to you in your mind.[14] First spackle the holes, apply fresh paint, new wall paper. Yes, cover the blemishes, cover the room with newness, make it look fresh and clean. You stand back and look at your accomplishments, you are pleased, then you see something that was missed. The paint along the top of the wall and ceiling did not come out right; that's okay, you can just put on some paper edging, this will cover that blemish. Your child comes into the room with a toy and scratches the wall, you add more paint and more wall paper. A chair is set too close to the wall and rubs the wall, causing another blemish. You add more paint, more wall paper. You see the patches you have made over time in the room, it doesn't look right, you apply new wall paper. The wall paper is out of style, you paint the room again. Layer after layer of coverings, you apply over time; each covering, hiding the defect beneath.

I hope you are beginning to see the picture of what is being done to the room. You would say that the reason you make these changes is because of your love of beauty, to ensure your own comfort, the comfort of others that enter into the room. I will tell you that I understand this desire. I understand and can empathize with your actions. Those

---

[14]   In this section, I try to summarize and provide a simplified explanation of what I received in lessons from Rich. He has reviewed these words and has assisted in clarifying some of the misconceptions I originally held.

actions are probably the correct action for the wall, but beneath those repairs, the original defect still exists.

The next question, "What do you do when the blemish is on your heart?" "Right there," he said, as he tapped his fingers on my chest, "what do you do to cover this blemish, and that thought on your mind, what is it that you do to hide it, that others do not see?" Yes, you go about life, still hanging the wall paper and spreading paint to cover the wounds and blemishes so that others will not be able to see the imperfections of self. So many coverings, so many, that eventually the true self is no longer visible, just a shell covered with paint and wall paper. Beneath the coverings, old wounds fester, the infection spreading through the body, we grow weak from the infectious attack, we respond with more paint and wall paper.

I hope that I have made my point sufficiently enough for you to understand the wall paper concept, and how it is being used in this story of evolution. I strive to see myself in that room, painting and hanging wall paper. In that revelation to self, hopefully I have looked at myself deeply to recognize each single self-blemish that I have worked to cover. If I can see it, then there is something that I can do with it, and I will be able to move forward to a better understanding of self. If I do not see it, then I must look harder. They are there, beneath multiple layers of wall paper. I must grab my paint scraper, start peeling away the old layers of paint and paper, remove those layers, pulling each layer away, until I reach the original wall. Find the original defect, and then I may work to fix it, to bring the festering wound to the light, to give it attention. Cleanse it, treat it, that it may heal.

THE STORYTELLER

I worked to manage my pride; to take a path to prove something to others or even myself of my own self-worth, or to convince someone of something true or perceived of my own self-image. It was down this path that I had to venture. I think of the words, "How can you ever know the 'with' if you have not experienced the 'without'?" Perhaps it is something that I could apply here, as it was down this path that I was able to experience some of the most complex of emotions and learn the meaning of without.

I have told many stories during my life to family and friends, and have often found difficulty in separating the facts from fiction. Yes, it is true, the exact stories told then may not have been as exciting as they could be, so the storyteller added a bit of filler to make the story more attractive to the listener. I cannot say that every story that I told then was false, any more than I could say they were exactly true. What I can admit is that some stories were true, some "decorated," and some were simply not told. Of all of these stories, they have all been told so many times that they have become real, and the untold stories have become a distant memory, hardly recallable. This is the trouble with pride. Pride is the hardest of the deadly sins to resolve, as to do so you must work to understand self and become humble, while at the same time not rejecting yourself. I understand that it is important to love one's self, such that one can love others more. It is complex because you do not love yourself and reject others, or elevate yourself up high at the cost of others. Being prideful often means "faultless," from the individual perspective. I can rejoice in my accomplishments and not suffer the negative side of pride, if I rejoice with humbleness and recognition of others that have contributed to that accomplishment.

Even as I write this, I am torn with the understanding of what this means. Let me give an example. I am so prideful that I cannot accept any form of criticism. If, in conversation, I perceive that someone is criticizing me, then I become upset and begin the process of defending my thoughts or actions. I start to counter discussions, perhaps raise my voice to be heard better or overpower another speaker. My responses are generally about all that I have done for others as pure sacrifice. I seek confirmation of that sacrifice and acknowledgment from others of both my sacrifice and accomplishments. This then escalates and turns into criticism and perceived attacks on others. Others take offense and retaliate, one word leads to others, and then someone is hurt. The negative energies smile on what they have encouraged to happen. They grab me by the shoulder and whisper in my ear, my wrath increases as these thoughts escalate, "I am right, they are wrong, look at how ignorant they are, I must respond to their lack of willingness to listen.

I raise my voice louder and overpower them. I must get mad; I must prove that I am right!"

THE ENERGIES OF EARTH

So, looking back I realize that I detested myself so much, and fell deeper and deeper into the depths of hell itself. I would soon come to realize that you did not need to die to go to hell. Hell, originally a Greek creation, is on earth, and earth belongs to the negative energies, or so it would seem at times. To verify this latter fact, I would review the text of the Book of Robes, and within that text I would discover the truth that others seemed to ignore. It is in Luke 4:5–7:

> *The devil led him up to a high place and showed him in an instant all of the kingdoms of the world. And he said to him, "I will give you all their authority and splendor, for it has been given to me, and I can give it to anyone I want to. So if you worship me, it will all be yours."*

From that verse I deduce that hell is on earth, and from other information that I have read or have been told, we choose to be here. The quote above is only a part of Luke, and I have also been told not to restrict myself to chapter and verse and not to make any decision on that part as each verse builds on the information of that which precedes it. Later, in the chapter, "In God's Service," I will talk more about this part of Luke and its meaning. For now, I just want to point out that we are here by our choice. Both positive and negative energies exist here, and that is a part of the plan. Freedom of choice requires that there are alternatives from which to choose, and thus we are cleansed of our memories so that we may experience that capability to choose, based on our own desire. Few, if any, carry the memories of the other side and the plan that we developed. One that did have those memories and is discussed in the Christian Bible and Jewish Torah is King Solomon.

This wisdom and greatness is reviewed, as referenced in 1 Kings 3:7–15 (NIV):

Now, O Lord my God, you have made your servant King in place of my father David. But I am only a little child and do not know how to carry out my duties. Your servant is here among the people you have chosen, a great people, too numerous to count or number. So give your servant a discerning heart to govern your people and to distinguish between right and wrong. For who is able to govern this great people of yours? The Lord was pleased that Solomon had asked for this. So God said to him, "Since you have asked for this and not for long life or wealth for yourself, nor have asked for the death of your enemies but for discernment in administering justice, I will do what you have asked. I will give you a wise and discerning heart, so that there will never have been anyone like you, nor will there ever be. Moreover, I will give you what you have not asked for—both riches and honor—so that in your lifetime you will have no equal among kings. And if you walk in my ways and obey my statutes and commands as David you father did, I will give you a long life." Then Solomon awoke—and he realized it had been a dream.

Further as referenced in 1 Kings 4:29 (NIV):

God gave Solomon wisdom and very great insight, and a breath of understanding as measureless as the sand on the seashore.

It is a summary of his wisdom, wisdom that comes from understanding.

The pain and suffering of many have led some to deny the very existence of God. Why? The rationale seems to be based on the fact that a good God would not allow bad things to happen to good people. So if bad things happen, it is because either God does not exist or God is not good. If God is not good, then the information in the Book of Robes about God is not true, so that leads to the conclusion that God does not exist. Sorry, I cannot subscribe to that position. The first and foremost truth for me is that God is. The second is that given that God is, and that God is good, then God gives his love freely. The last truth is that given God exists, and that God is love, then the works of the Book of Robes that attribute destruction and death to God cannot be true. What follows then is the search for the real truth. The truth is that I must cling to God and work to understand what it is that has put me in this place and time. I must continue to look deeper into the lessons of history, no matter where they are written. I must continue to look deeper into myself, to open the wounds that have been covered and have festered with infection for so many years. I must open the wounds, cleanse them, and by giving them attention, help them to heal.

CHANGE

I think about two conflicting and parallel feelings that defined my youth: fear and understanding. I would seek to understand others and hope that they would develop an understanding of me. My fear is that they would develop an understanding of me. If they really knew me, what would they really think of me? If they understood my fears, then they may lose respect for me, or I would lose respect for them for invading my privacy.

I struggled to understand myself. I struggled to understand others, the world, and the universe. The basic thing that I began to understand was that I did not enjoy being alone. I did not enjoy being afraid. I wanted to break out of the shell that bound me so tightly. There were those there at the time that would not be able to understand my struggle. I was just the smart-ass from algebra class. There were others that I did not know or pay enough attention to know. These were the gentle people, the ones who sought to understand, that would have shared more if given the chance. I did not know them, I was afraid to try.

As I look back at that time, I clearly see the movements I made to exit my shell. I wanted more and sought to achieve my goals. I tried hard to talk to young ladies that impressed me so much. Some I had ignored earlier, but now I sought their company. No, I did not generally succeed, but I sought to try. There was one, a dear friend that did not know how much I cherished her friendship. I cherished it so much, but I could do nothing to help it grow. One morning in study hall, sitting across from me at the table, she said, "If you were to lose weight I would be glad to go out with you." I responded, "Who is asking?" I am sorry for that cold response. I loved her friendship, but much to my regret I lost it that day. I understand that it was necessary to break any potential bound that would hold me there in that place. I love Mimi and my family more than I can possibly express, but the memories of those days and words spoken still bother my heart.

The next, a new friend, one who worked at a local fast food restaurant, whom I only met there, but with whom I shared many long conversations. She would often take a break when I arrived, and we would share a few moments of friendly conversation. She was a beautiful person who helped me grow; I can hardly express my thanks and admiration enough.

Finally, there was a beautiful young lady with an amazing personality. At first there was only gentle teasing, but then a fondness began to grow and a friendship of such depth that I cherish it even now. What you must realize is that I did not believe in myself and did not think I could ever give her what she needed. I knew that I must move on, and away from those there, there at that place and that time. It was not my place, it was just a path to knowing myself and part of the anchors that I must separate from my life. It is okay for me to remember her and love her still. I can see her smile, the brightness of her eyes, the joy of a reunion after months of separation. I hope she finds this paragraph and knows that I am talking about her. I hope that I will be able to see her smile as she reads these words and we share, at that moment, this memory together.

So, what does all this mean in the context of this story? How much is true and how much is "decorated"? What I can tell you is that what I present in this book is meant to be the most exact and accurate account of my past. For me it must be presented in the most accurate light, as it is a part of the cleansing of old wounds. Yet, more than that, for you it must be an account of where I have been contrasted to where I am today, and then where I hope to be tomorrow. For this to occur, I must acknowledge to you that I have suffered from pride and have sought various ways to fulfill my desire that others would see me in a different light than I saw myself. This person that I wanted them to see was that mythical man from the training of my youth.

TRANSITIONS FROM THEN TO NOW

In the late 1990s, I tried once again to find my way closer to my spiritual side. I spoke with many about how there are times when we get on a path and proceed along that path with no control of its outcome. I have given multiple examples of those types of events.

In 1972, I graduated high school and applied to the University of Missouri, Rolla. I was accepted for admission that fall but would not get there. My parents separated at the end of 1971 and completed their divorce in the spring of 1972. They did not have the financial resources to assist me in college, and I was without the knowledge of student loans and other financial aid programs. The things that happened that fall and into the spring and summer of 1973 set me on the next path of my life. The first actions were designed to separate me from the anchors that held me in the small Missouri town of Marshall. The first event was the divorce of my parents. The second was an automobile accident that destroyed my car, which I cherished so much, and then finally there was an altercation with my best friend. Troubled and alone, I sought to change my life and meet new friends. I met two important people in the winter and spring of 1972. These two helped me understand myself more than anyone I had ever encountered. I enjoyed them and spent as much time as possible in their company. But this again was not the intended path, as still the pressure was there for me to do something else.

I sat outside on the step of my apartment house, looking to heaven, and I asked, "What now? What would you have me do?" How interesting the response: subtle, not direct. Would I completely understand it then? No, I would not, but reflecting on it many times since has given me strength in God's presence. What followed was confusing, as on the next day, while working in the checkout stand at the grocery store, a US Army recruiter walked up and asked me, as if we had talked many times before, "What time are you coming up to talk to me?" I looked at him, without really thinking, and replied, "In about an hour."

I struggle to find the period in time where the transition began. I might consider the point in 1972 when I was sitting on the step outside my apartment, or it may have been about three years ago when my son decided to start his own engineering company in Florida. Many times over the years, I acknowledge thoughts and feelings that convince me of the path that we follow in our lives. Circumstantial evidence, or just random thought, I rarely challenged the source of the information but accept the facts as they presented themselves to me.

It was during this period that Rich's nightmares became more extreme. They became so bad that he dropped to a level of fear and apprehension that eventually led to his inability to even step outside his home. He finally sought medical assistance and was put on medication to help him cope. He would call me and tell me of the attacks, and I would try to help him as best I could. My story was always about putting his faith in God and ignoring the negative forces that tormented him. He would say that there was no way that I could understand what he was going through. He spoke of visitations, visualizations, and conversations that were confusing to me. He stated that he would curl up in a fetal position, curled up tightly as they viciously attacked him. "Just get it over with," he would tell them. I told him he must fight back, pass them over to me, I was not afraid; I would gladly take them from him. He would look at me, deep pain in his eyes, and then simply reply, "You do not know of what you ask, it is nothing that I would willingly give to anyone, even if I could." I will go into this more later when I talk about the influences of negative energies. My point is that things were happening that go far beyond my physical understanding and would be perceived as impossible to occur within the rational mind. In trying to help him, I was arrogant and once again refer back to the seven deadly sins and how I have lived each and every one. In this case, I fell to pride and wrath. Pride in myself to imagine what I dreamed could be done, and anger about my inability to change things. I would get so impatient, so frustrated in working with him. I could not know but thought I did understand and knew what he should do. It was frustrating that he would not do what I asked.

As I type this, I suddenly realize the answer to most of my pleas for assistance, even my plea for help with my poor stricken cow. God's response is not always visible unless we open our hearts and eyes. I asked for help, he sent my brother first, and when she was comfortable for me, she was allowed to be taken.

THE COLOR BLUE

When we are born, we are born into a life of suffering. We now transition into a time where our reality is a function of time. It is this reality that we have no memory of what we are and of home. Possibly, in the first few months, the memories remain, but they slowly fade and are replaced with what we experience in this lifetime. You could think in terms of a baby's eyes, so blue at birth and then changing to their true color. The blue must come from the memory of home. We are surrounded by blue, by the essence of God's love. You may wonder about the truth of this thought, whether God's love is represented by the color blue. How interesting to consider it. To wonder of this truth is like realizing how blind one can be to the truth. All that is around us, all that appears to us, is a gift from God. These sights, sounds, smells, feelings, tastes, all of these we are unable to absorb. Close your eyes for a moment and meditate. How did you feel? What did you think? Did you begin to understand the color blue? Perhaps you should try it again. Do not bow your head; instead hold your head straight. Sit straight in your chair, grasp your hands together, and hold them to your abdomen. Clear your mind, do not try to answer the question, do not talk, think blue, and listen.

Oh! I follow my own advice, how beautiful, how serene. I could only imagine that you felt something close to my feelings. As I breathed in, I thought of the blue, pulled in by my lungs, flowing in through my nostrils, absorbing into my body. Serenity flooded through my mind, calm, peaceful, a feeling of . . . But what did you feel? I don't want to lead you to a conclusion, instead I would ask that you complete the sentence. Perhaps later I will tell you the remainder. But for now, it is time to take a break and meditate on blue. Let God give you the answer. What is the significance of blue?

THE LESSONS

When we think of the challenges of the flesh, we should take a moment to review history. This history is documented in various religious texts including the Christian Bible and Jewish Torah. The history of man was wrought with pain and struggle, religious sacrifice, human torture, slavery, misguidance, and an abundance of rules.

I am not a religious scholar; though I have studied the Bible, I cannot claim to be an expert. What I have done is study the historical information that is presented, and I have asked questions. In response to my questions, I have come to a certain set of conclusions that I call my facts. Above I summarized my view of the information that is provided in the Biblical Old Testament. Now, I will go further and state that God saw this suffering and sent his prophets to proclaim the coming of a savior for mankind. I understand that the savior was a messenger of extreme importance, one who would teach the purity of God's love and then endure suffering that is beyond our own understanding. We have read the information; we have seen the multiple movies that have attempted to capture what occurred. *The Passion of Christ*, by Mel Gibson, in my opinion, was one of the best portrayals of the final days of his suffering, but still it could not capture the depth of the suffering and demonstration of God's love for us all. Was the suffering worth it? Look at him there, white bones showing through the torn flesh. Tortured, tormented, and held in contempt and disdain; all that he taught was thrown aside such that he could demonstrate the final levels of God's love. The interpretations of his years of teaching, healing, miracles, parables, all of the writings and sermons try to capture the full meaning of his life and message, but then the ultimate irony that I perceive is that the purity of the message that he delivered to all of those who surrounded him and all who would read the stories for two thousand years was lost. Was it worth it? Did his life, did his death, make a difference?[15]

So how was his life different from our own? For one, he was sent here with a special mission. That mission was to teach the purity of God's love, that from his example, we might learn and understand the complete depth of God's love. He taught many things to include understanding, love, caring, and sharing. He showed what was possible when a person had total faith in God. He spoke in parables, always teaching, always showing, but never directing. To direct would be to forfeit free will, and as stated earlier, free will is a gift from God. I have asked many questions and have entered into much dialog on the subject. Was Jesus the son of God? The answer was yes. Was he the only son of God? The answer was presented by direction to look for the answer in Genesis 6:2. There it actually references that there are many sons of God. I then understand that we are all sons and daughters of God. But that may be hard for you to accept, as it suggests we all would be somewhat equal to God, and that would be blasphemous. More blasphemous, from a Christian perspective, would be to challenge the virgin birth of Jesus.

---

[15]   In the fall of 2009, at Rich's home in was "in spirit" several hours. It was an intense training session for me, first alone and then later with Mimi and Sumer. It was during this time that Sumer was told to pass to me the information from an earlier conversation he had with her. One of these was my true name. At the end of the session, he had one of the most painful returns to body that I had ever witnessed. In anticipation, I had moved close to him, and then all of a sudden, his body shot backward, rigid, out of his chair. I grabbed onto him as he thrashed, Sumer holding tightly to him as well. For several minutes we held on as he cried in pain. After what seemed like forever, he relaxed and Sumer went into the bathroom and fixed a hot bath for him to soak out the pain. She took him to the tub, and he stepped in, clothes and all. She said he wanted to talk to me. I went in; he looked at me and asked, "Was it worth it?" I told him this was so difficult to answer, as the answer seemed selfish. How could I say yes, considering the pain I witnessed of his return? It was like saying that the crucifixion of Christ was worth it. He looked at me and said, "Would you say that Jesus went through all of that for nothing, that it meant nothing for anyone, that it made no difference?"

But for the leaders of the Christian movement to explain the divine nature of his mission, it was necessary to put his creation into some miraculous event, an event that only God could perform (again, back to learning by reference).

If you look close enough, the concept of miraculous creation can be explained by the gods of Greek and Norse lore. The heroes of many of those stories, including Hercules and Achilles, were all of virgin or divine birth, where the gods lay with their mothers, who birthed a special person that was half god and half man (historians will challenge my facts; understand I am not trying to be exact, just to introduce a thought). Would it only make sense that those same authors, writing of the birth of Jesus, would come to the same type of explanation of his birth? We cannot know the real truth, in terms of genetic testing, to determine if Joseph was his biological father, but even if we did, would it really matter?

Once again, another explanation presented to me was that if everything that we read within the Book of Robes happened exactly as told, it is hard to imagine that the Jewish faith would still exist. That it does exist does not suggest that something did not happen, it only suggests that the exact details of what occurred are obscured with different interpretations and manipulation of information. Sometimes, this type of transcription can occur simply by the lack of understanding of the individual who provides witness to the fact. For example, if you interview ten people, standing on a corner, all seeing the same accident, you will get ten separate understandings of the event. It would not be a result of people trying to obscure the truth, it would only be their interpretation of the truth based on what they saw and heard, applied against their reference database. This latter part of interpretation is very significant in our human history. We spend a significant amount of time looking at the past and the interpretations of others, often not fully comprehending the impact of the individual reference database to the information that is provided.

SMALL ACTIONS MAKE A DIFFERENCE

To understand where I am, and where I am going, I need to take a moment to align myself to the spiritual universe. There are many that can help me achieve a path to alignment. Spiritualists, shamans, and mental studies of Buddhism are examples. The path to true alignment comes from within. Mixed with desire, the path may lead to a fulfillment that I have never experienced or understood in terms of my experience within my reference database. For example, it was suggested to me that I find a place of positive energy within my home, or perhaps outside. This is a place where I may experience God's gifts to me. These gifts include the rays of sunshine, birds singing, water trickling, and the breeze rustling the tree leaves. I take the moment to experience nature with my senses. Feeling, hearing, and seeing each of the natural gifts placed there by God, not by man. I experience this during a short walk in the morning or evening, or I just stop on the way from my door to my car and breathe in the positive energy from God. I stop, standing straight, head up, gazing around to see at all that is natural, or close my eyes and listen to the sounds of nature, filtered from cars and doors and other man-made noise. I focus my hearing toward the sounds of birds, squirrels, insects, and rustling trees. I breathe in the fresh air, slow full breaths, first one, then another, and another. Several breaths I take, while exhaling, visioning in my mind the exhalation of negative energy, and while inhaling feeling the positive energy of God flow into my soul. All of this transpires in less than a minute. Refreshed, I go on with my day. Read again these steps, they did not say I must spend an hour, a day, a week, no, it was just a few breaths, less than a minute, each and every day. You would then ask, as I asked, how could so little make such a difference? The answer was provided to me as stated below:

> He:[16] *Do you know how big an acorn seed is? Not big, food of squirrels. So small, so small, even one is not sufficient for a squirrel, yet that seed, it becomes a majestic oak, with a huge canopy a hundred feet high and sixty feet wide. It does not happen overnight. It is amazing that a little love and tenderness*

---

[16] Rich "in spirit" state two.

can grow to its own magnificence. Change is good, little by little, bit by bit the acorn becomes an oak. How does such a little thing make such a difference? Let an ant bite you on the thigh (he laughs), so little, so small, so insignificant, how can it make any difference? Then, let the ant bite you on the thigh, and see if it has a difference. So much, so little, the ant. Have you ever thought about the significance of a hair on the head? That one little hair, how insignificant, pull it out and see the significance it makes.

He: Do you think the spiritual world will treat you differently? The little exercise makes a difference. One minute, the ant, the insignificance. How can the one hair on your head make such a difference? Have you ever wondered about that? It does make a difference.

It was shortly after receiving this information that I sat in my office, working, when an extraordinary pain wrenched through the lower right side of my abdomen. The pain shot around to my back, I broke into a sweat, and nausea swept through me like a tornado. I could not recall such a feeling. I immediately thought of a kidney stone, I had heard how painful they were and had witnessed my wife suffer through such torment years earlier. I thought I was tougher than this and that I could endure, but the pain worsened, and I feared that I would faint. I took a deep breath, begged God for strength, and left the office. I went straight to my doctor's office, where I was given pain medication and a filter to catch the offending stone, and then I drove home to ride this ordeal to its conclusion. It would take four days for the stone to pass, each movement causing excruciating agony. When it finally passed, it was so small, so tiny, I could hardly imagine how it could have had such significance on me. When people asked me how I felt, I responded, "Blessed." I thanked God for the lesson, a lesson of extreme importance, the importance of understanding that little things, and thus little actions, can make a huge difference.

Understanding Negative
Influences

Another thing I try to understand is the point where one third of the angels left God's side. I present a summary of what I think; I understood that there came a time in the presence of God that certain angels felt themselves equal to him, and they challenged him to the right to live differently. The leader of this group is known within religious circles as Satan (and perhaps other names such as Lucifer). This group of angels, that consisted of one third of all angels in heaven, decided to depart of their own free will. I do not think that God cast them out or that he would prevent them from returning home. "God loves all of his children, even the ones that make him cry." It is possible that within the Book of Robes, that Genesis presents this part of the story in the story of Adam and Eve, possibly another of the many parables that are told within this book and other such books of the same heritage. It is also possible that in addition to the introduction to the creation of the negative forces, within this section we are also introduced to the seven deadly, or cardinal, sins. Once again, I am only sharing what I understand.

Regardless of the exact course that was taken and documented, the negative energies reside on the earthly plane, and under Satan's leadership, they provide negative influences to the people of this physical world.

Negative influences work to disguise their presence around you. It is to their benefit for you to believe that negative actions come from other things or people around you. Yet the majority of the time, the negative influences are acting directly on you. This can be described in the same way as a leech attaching itself to your arm. There may be those of you who read these words that will correct me on the exact biological nature of the leech; however, as a brief overview, a leech will inject into your skin its saliva, which causes a deadening effect to the area where the leech would bite you. This prevents you from feeling the leech's presence. Should that chemical not be present, you would feel the pain of the leech when it attaches to your arm and take action to remove it, thus preventing it from getting the nourishment it seeks.

Negative energies serve in the same way as the leech. They disguise their presence such that you do not interfere with their work, instead nourishing their needs. It is hard for you to avoid the effects of negative energies when you don't know they are there. Later I will discuss the depth of the power that may be applied, power such that a person may believe they are really concerned and acting on behalf of others, but may just be feeding the negative energies.

Let us take a moment and consider a story as presented to me.

> *He:*[17] *Two men are floating in a metaphorical pond of life. Each is attacked by the leeches that reside within it. Over time, they both begin to feel the influences associated with the bloodletting that is occurring. One day, the men begin to question the feelings on themselves. Why are we sluggish? Why do we feel our life leaving? They say a prayer that God would help them with their unknown ailment. On one man, the relief of mitigation comes. And in one fell swoop, the leeches are gone, and he continues to float along. However, not long after the exodus of leeches, more begin to reattach themselves, and soon the man is back to the same predicament that he was in. The other man is given a gift of endurance. Instead of the leeches being washed away, instead, an angel makes his skin immune to the saliva of the leeches. The next thing the man knows, he is nearly drowned in the horrid pain of so many leeches biting upon him. He struggles as he tears each and every leech off his body, all the time wondering what he did to deserve such anguish, thinking all the time, why it is the man next to him felt no such pain. Through the strength of endurance, he is able to rid himself of the leeches, and more*

---

17   Lessons from Rich over the phone; I do not think he was "in spirit."

importantly, it could be justifiably said that he will continue to float along the rest of his life, relatively leech free. For now, he knows the pain of the leech and can remove it as it happens. Which blessing is greater?

THE ACCIDENT

It is June 1996. My wife and I took a cleaning job on the weekend. Our daughter was at the house, and our son was working at a local gas station. Early that afternoon, I received a page to call the house, it included a suffix 911. I called once, twice, three times without success. I continued to try and then received a call from my stepfather. He stated I needed to call my daughter. I called again, and she told me that her brother had been in an auto accident. He was in the emergency room of a nearby hospital. I gathered our things and told Mimi that we had to go. She said we were not finished, but I repeated that we had to go. You must understand that I did not want to frighten her by saying what had happened. She gathered her things, and we quickly left for the hospital. I was nervous and scared and finally told her we had to get to the hospital, that Rich was there and I did not know more than that. We arrived at the emergency room, and the triage nurse quickly calmed me by letting me know that, though he had a few injuries, he was okay. We went to his side, embraced him, and asked what happened. He was passing through an intersection when another vehicle had suddenly turned into his lane, and he ran into it head-on. Yes, he had injuries to his back, head, arms, and legs. Most of these were invisible to the eye. We did not understand the significance of a closed head injury and what it meant in terms of loss of short-term memory or periods of anger or hostility. We would eventually learn, but what we would not know for many years was that the negative energies would come to him and begin an attack, first as a friend, but ultimately as the evil and dangerous element it is. Those attacks would last for over thirteen years.

PHYSICAL CONTROL

I looked closely at the history of he that came before as documented in the Book of Robes and tried to understand the temptation offered to him on the mountain. What was significant about this was how Satan visited him and the offer that was made. The gist of the offer was that Satan would give him the world if he would just acknowledge Satan as his leader, rejecting God for Satan. He said, bow before me and all of this will be yours. Well, we know the outcome of that offer, and there was no second offer documented to others that I am aware of, but that does not mean it has not happened; by Rich's account, during the fall of 2008, he was given the same offer, that if he were to choose Satan, then he would be given the world.[18] His response was, "I don't want it." He was given a second option, that he would receive all that he ever needed or desired. His answer: "I already have all of this." The third option presented was then, "I will take your wife." Whereupon, within the vision that was given, the demon grabbed her and began pulling her through the floor as he grabbed onto her body and fought to save her and pull her back to his side.

He had many such encounters with these demonic negative energies. They would torment him, and he would beg for God's assistance to block this torment. These energies only mocked him in his pleas for God to destroy them. They said, "God would no more destroy me than you, as he loves all of his children, even the ones that make him cry."

So what is it that these negative energies desire? I could just cut to the chase and state that they desire to destroy God, though it may not be God they hope to destroy, but something else, perhaps man. They do

---

[18] This should not be interpreted that I consider that Rich is/was the second coming of Christ, only that there are those that are on a path that is chosen and dictated by God. Their plan is to have no plan, but support the plan of the father. When this happens, the negative energies are given freedom to change that course of action if they can. When I think of this, it is an option that they have for each of us. I beg my guides to help keep me on the path of God.

not seem to love God and therefore wish his destruction.[19] I don't know what destruction means or if that is even possible, but I understand that they work this destruction one soul at a time, hence the destruction of man. If they can block a soul from returning home, then they are en route to achieving their desired outcome. The method is very simple. Create an attraction to the world for each person that anchors him or her to the world, blocking the return home.

I struggle to write this, as it is simply my interpretation of what I think I understand. I do not have the task of instruction, in fact I do not have a task at all, but I have the desire to share with you what I think I understand and how I use it to help me on my path. I understand that I have free will, freedom of choice, and that this choice is a gift from God. I think I understand that if I exercise that choice in a wrong way, it can only serve to assist the negative energies in the accomplishment of their ultimate goal. I do not choose to do that. So, given a choice of service, I choose to apply my service to God.

My goal is to separate myself from anchors that may bind my soul to the earth and hence free my soul to return home at the end of this lifetime or the next, though that is mostly unrealistic, the thought that I could return home and know without restriction the love of God. My hope is that at least one of you will gain an understanding of what I am saying, and from there be touched with this such that you work toward the same path as me. That one touching one, and that one touching one, over the course of eternity will touch an infinite number of souls, and that infinite number will find their way back home to God.

---

[19]   This whole concept is so hard to understand. I present an alternate thought on this later. That thought is that they do what they do because of their love for God, because of their love for man, and to support the overall plan of freedom of choice, and that by overcoming that negative influence that we will be able to ultimately and completely understand God's love and by doing so, understand how to love.

THE OFFICE

I walked into an office area this morning, a small space, perhaps twenty-four feet by thirty feet. Within this space were eight cubicles, each cubicle roughly eight-by-eight. There were no windows in this space. The doors were shut; each space was cluttered and the atmosphere heavy. Fluorescent lighting and the smell of stale coffee and waste baskets weighed heavily in the small space. The people working there were stressed, their frustrations were vocalized regularly. They were eager to swear and criticize. I sat in the room for an hour, and at the end of that hour I was so drained of energy. I could feel the negative forces reaching out to grab and pull. I understand they grow in that room. They grow because they are fed. They feed from the stress and the negative emotions of the people. With each complaint or criticism, they gain more strength and more power. They use this to encourage more of the same. I could feel them on my own shoulders, trying to encourage me to join in the turmoil. I recognized that I must resist, but I understood that resistance is not just ignoring the issue, or fighting them, but looking for options that will weaken them.

I look at this and always remember that all of us have a choice. We have to choose to do what we do, whatever that is, including the choice to hate and criticize. It is not my job to force people to act the way that I desire them to act. It is their choice to make. Even the messengers from God will not dictate to a person what they must or must not do. They only deliver a message, often hidden within a small story or parable that is open to interpretation. If you seek meaning in that parable, then you will find the answer that you desire to find. I am not a messenger; of this I have received multiple reminders. I am a listener. I open my heart to hear their messages. Because I care for you, I share what I know. Because I care for them, those in the room, I sought to give them advice, advice on how they could improve their environment, should they so choose. So, to help them, I encouraged those within the office to find something positive to add to the area. I suggested they add plants, pictures, or other happy things to the decoration of the room. I think they could open the doors to create a path to the light. Yes, some tried to add family photos to give them energy. I just don't think they took time to look at those photos and thank God for all that they have. The photos were not used as reminders of his glory, only what they gave up by being in that job, at that place, at that time. To have positive energy within the room, the occupants must bring it there. The positive energy will grow if they want it to. Yet they cannot just want, they must act. To act, they must choose to act. To choose, they must understand they have a choice, and hence my message to them.

THE POWER TO CONTROL

Now, I need to share a warning with you. I, and you, do not have the power to do battle with the forces of negative energies. It is not a game to play, and it is not even close to what you might see on some glorified television show where people go out and challenge the forces of the spiritual world. If you are blessed with any level of protection, you must realize that those you encounter on a daily basis might not have that same level of protection or resistance. Anything can happen at any time, that may be a part of your plan, or it may be an alteration of the plan. Whatever the case, consider this: you cannot do battle with negative energies, in terms of your understanding of "battle"; you can only hurt yourself or others around you. The only thing that I believe you can do is focus your energies on God's love, and try to return that love to him and those around you. Think about the impact of your words before speaking, so you may reduce the regret of those words after they are spoken. Study the teaching of he who was sent here to help each of us, and attempt to understand what was truly spoken, not what was perceived to be understood.

FEAR

What is fear? I could define fear as an emotion of many levels that results in anxiety, nervousness, and regret. But let's look at this differently. Consider that you are cooking an egg on a stove, and you put on an apron. Someone asks why you wear the apron; the answer you give is that you are afraid the oil will splatter on you. But is that really fear? Consider another example, where you stop to fill up the car with gas and someone asks, "Why are you filling the car now?" and you answer, "I was afraid I would run out of gas." But that does not seem to be the correct meaning either. So what is the real meaning? You use the word every day of your life, yet you may not know the meaning. So consider the last time you were afraid. When was it? What was the feeling? Do you know what caused it?

Attempt to describe fear to someone that does not know its meaning; explain it, not using acronyms, but more directly as a function of what it is. It may be difficult to do this, as we have basically applied fear to everything that would invoke even the slightest level of negative emotion, overusing the word and reducing its meaning to something less than its original intent.

So why is this important? Well, consider "love," another word that has been reduced in everyday use to a word of degraded meaning. We love everything; I love this beer, I love this wine, I love this car, I love you. Each of these uses has no more weight with the individual than any other. We say we love God, but in reality, because we have degraded the word, we have degraded God as well; we do not truly understand its meaning. Consider, is your spouse the best thing that ever happened to you? How many have you told this to? This person is your soul mate.

But how do you treat this best thing that ever happened to you? Is that the same way you treat God?

Let's go back and once again consider fear. Have you ever experienced true fear? If so, could you explain it? Imagine that an angel sat down in front of you and asked, "What is fear, how does it feel?" What would you tell them? How would it be that they do not know fear but you do? Is that possible?

Fear could be explained with a series of words or statements, such as cold, alarming, anxious, shaky, terrifying, no control, intimidating, heart-stopping emotion, a sick feeling in the abdomen, anxiety driven by the thought of pending pain or loss. To expand the latter, it could be described as a condition that results in the thought of losing something that is of ultimate importance to you. The greater the importance, the more difficult the loss, the higher the level of fear that is encountered. Consider these examples: I am afraid of losing my car, my job, my house, my life, my mother, my wife. This puts the complete description of fear on the single basis of loss. I think back on my fear on the farm. Why was I afraid? The answer can be understood when reviewing the story of the hen and her brood. Animals can inflict pain, I had experienced that pain and did not want to repeat the process. So ultimately, the feeling of fear results from the expectation of pain, or loss of something important. I have often overestimated the probability of loss and, given that overestimation, have felt much more fear than necessary.

> "It was middle of the night, I was alone in my room. The night air was cold, I shivered as I sat up in bed, staring into the dark and listening. What woke me? A sound, what sound? I listened intently, unable to see through the darkness. Was that a footstep, the creak of the wood floor from the weight of someone creeping down the hall? I listened more intensely, there was another sound, breathing. Sweat broke on my brow, my heart pounded in my chest. Yes, there was something there, what should I do? I looked left and right for any kind of weapon, should I run, hide, then . . . no, this is not acceptable, stop, clear my mind. I threw back the blankets and leapt from the bed, flinging on the lights as I rushed into the hall, to confront . . . nothing. Nothing was there, just nothing but me with my wildly racing heart and vivid imagination."

Returning to the question asked, what is fear? The reason it is asked is to understand the human condition that creates fear. I watched a character in a movie, re-enacting the events of World War II; the character said that to be effective as a soldier, you must accept the fact that you are already dead. It sounded so simple to me, because if you could accept that, then there could be no potential of loss, as all that could be lost was already gone, and thus the soldier could be fearless, as fear cannot exist in an environment where there can be no loss. That was only an example, I do not assert that one should assume one is already dead to live life fearlessly, that is certainly not my point. The point I am making is that for me to reduce my own anxiety, or fear, it is necessary for me to understand the root cause of fear. Because I exist as human, I cannot eliminate fear altogether, but if I understand what causes it, I can modify my behavior such that it does not control me.

The discussion of fear came up, and the question was asked by the angel, what is fear, would you explain it to me? The question was perhaps rhetorical, but it was also explained that the angels do not know fear.[20] Angels were created by God. They stand by God and know, without condition, the level of God's love. They have seen you come and go across multiple lifetimes, they know you, they know your soul. They do not experience pain, they do not experience loss, there is nothing to lose. So fear is a creation of man, we create fear by binding ourselves to our earthly anchors. And when we have bound ourselves sufficiently, we can then experience fear, the feeling of what will happen if we lose that to which we are bound. Human nature? Yes, we fear the loss of our loved ones, that we will never see them again. Yet, to really lose them, the impossible must happen, and that would be the death of God, and that could never happen, period. God is forever, and therefore our souls are forever, so we never lose anyone from a spiritual perspective.

Unfortunately, in our physical world, we do not remember the spiritual world. Because we are human, we have created fear. Fear is tied to the feeling that we will lose something that is important to

[20] Lessons from Rich, "in spirit," possibly state one.

us. You are afraid to get a spot on your shirt; why? Because someone would look at you and think less of you? Whatever the reason, big or small, our feeling of loss is real, and our feelings of fear are understood.

BELIEFS AND DESIRE

Notes from his workbook:

"The one who sits on the universal plane, breathes into the heart of man, a flame of desire. Those who accept, experience its joy, those who do not, experience its pain, pain that is the lack of desire."

Within me there exists the "soul wish" of desire, the desire for God to assist me with my weight problem. From that desire, I made a request and God provided me the answer, the solution to this problem. With that solution came the flame, the flame to ignite and transform the soul's desire to the physical desire, the desire to achieve the results from the solution to the question asked. That solution led to the physical choice to follow the rule set presented to me, rigorously, to achieve the results that I desire. From this I am able to experience the joy of that desire, to see daily the results of following the solution, to see my weight drop daily, to see the results in the fit of my clothes, the looseness of my watch, the acknowledgment of family, friends, and associates that view this transformation. I feel better. My mind is more clear, I take my morning walks, follow my fast, love more openly, criticize less, and rejoice in my new-found energy.

Do you believe in angels? Do you believe in demons, ghost, spirits? It really does not matter whether you do or not. The fact is, they believe in you! When one of these elements chooses to speak to you or visit you, they do not ask if you believe in them. They choose what they do, it is their choice, not yours. Whether or not you believe in angels, are able to hear the angels, or are able to receive a message from them is your choice, it is up to you. It is a gift from God, that gift of choice, free will. I have been blessed with information from the angels, information that permits me a better understanding of God and our role here on earth. I have been challenged in my mind on what I should do with this information. Why is this information provided to me and not others? When I asked this question, the following dialog ensued:

> *He:[21] Do you think yourself blessed, that because you sit close to the shepherd that the shepherd loves you more?*

> *Me: I think it so, considering the blessings that have been bestowed upon me.*

> *He: The blessings you receive are there because you ask for them. They are always there. They are there for others who desire to receive them, others who listen. If the others do not hear, it is because of their choice not to do so.*

It was a quiet fall weekend, not much occurring, and Mimi had left that Saturday for Baltimore to spend time with the grandchildren. I had heard from my mother that my brother would be visiting his son. My brother had not called to speak to me about this, but I understood the reason. That reason was simple, whether he saw me or not was up to my nephew, he did not feel it his choice. I understood this, I don't have to agree with the approach, but that is his way and that is okay with me. In any case, my nephew, being thoughtful, called and asked if I cared to come up for Sunday dinner. Though I have been on a strict fast, I agreed quickly, why would I not do this? I can still observe my fast and enjoy their company. It is family time, I need to make up or remove the wall paper of the past where I ignored family and failed in my tasks as an uncle. I have never given my nieces and nephews the attention they deserve. I feel bad about that, but perhaps in time I can replace the past with the present.

I arrived and they commented on my weight loss, and then Rich called. He had been talking to Sissy and apparently she asked him a question,

---

[21] Rich, "in spirit," state two.

and the answer was causing her a great deal of pain. He was still in a spiritual state and said that I should call and talk to her when I got a moment. I asked if he wanted to speak with his uncle, and he said that would be nice. I then handed the phone to my brother, telling him that his nephew was in a spiritual state. Okay, you are right, that was probably not the correct thing to do at this time, to take him by surprise and introduce all of this at once into my nephew's home. Let me try to find an analogy, let's see, think about standing in a very dark room, perhaps for an extended period of time, and then suddenly someone turns on a massive spotlight, and then imagine your reaction. That may be the best that I can possibly compare this to, though I may ask them of this and see what their impression was; all that I am saying is that I did introduce him in this state to his uncle, and he greeted his uncle warmly over the phone and then told him how he wished he were there. He then stated that it would be nice if his uncle set a place for him at the table, and when taking dessert, it would be nice to be served a piece of that nice pie.

My nephew set the place at the table, next to my uncle, who throughout the meal left the plate unnoticed. I suggested that he put a meat ball there; he looked at me and grudgingly complied. We talked at length of my experiences, my desire to share with each of them that which had crossed my path. It was hard for them all to absorb, and I think that occasionally I may have ruffled a feather, one or two. Still you must understand the polite nature of my nephew and his wife, who would not say a word to hurt my feelings. I thank them for this even today. On my exit, my brother followed me to the truck and said that I was misinformed and that I surely talked too much or put too much emphasis on all of the information that I had received, or that this information could be coming from darkness not light. I looked at him and tried to explain the differences, but his mind was closed to listening, preferring to present me with the protection of an older brother. As for me, all was too new and I was much too inexperienced to effectively communicate what has occurred or to teach what I have come to understand.

I have to be careful in this area that I don't begin thinking that I have all of the knowledge, that I am the instructor. If I go down this path, then I have achieved no more than others around me. They have told me that I am not receiving information that is unique to me, only that it is provided because I ask, that it is available to all that ask. I start to say "but"; however, yesterday when I started a sentence with "but," he looked at me and said, "You like that word." I felt chastised. Why? Because it is the first word of an excuse, perhaps that is why I felt that way. I digress.

I left there feeling that I had left something undone. That is expected, it is evolution not revolution. The acorn does not turn into the oak in a day, it takes many days to germinate and years to grow to its full adult size. No, many times we look at the tree and think that it has reached all that is possible; still, if we drill into its base, we will see that it has grown every year since it first stuck itself out of the soil into the light. Why should we be different? Our lives, like the tree, grow every day. We grow in knowledge and experience. We expand. We spread our roots, seeking food and taking in the nourishment that is provided. There are trees that become dormant, that begin to die, and that struggle in their existence. That too is understood, it is not unlike any one of us. I may seem to ramble on, to go from one point to another. What I am trying to convey is that knowledge does not get delivered on a platter for us to absorb in one sitting, it comes one piece at a time, over time. It is our choice to receive that knowledge or to ignore it. One person's information may not be identical to another person's.

THE PORTRAIT

On another day, we were sitting together, and while in one of his many spiritual states, he drew the picture below.[22] We all sat and looked at this drawing, trying to see the intended picture. We looked at the drawing; he pointed out the barn, the sun, the fences, and the fields. As we reviewed the drawing and he led us through it, we could see each image so clearly. We discussed this picture, and he explained that you only see what you desire to see. Some may stand at the edge of the

---

22   This was the fall of 2009, referenced earlier. Rich is "in spirit" state two, but at times he seems to transition between state one and two.

farm, seeing the dusty road, ragged fence, and sagging barn and decide not to venture further. Others may see something different and choose to walk along the road to discover something they could not see from the outside.

I studied the picture closely, seeing a building, a fence, a road, crops in the back field, and the sun. I asked him why he drew it, what it meant. He looked at me and stated, "This is your farm, it is a portrait of you."

Later, he took the pen in hand again and drew another picture (not included). In this case, we looked at it and I said I could see an image of him, sitting there and smoking his cigar. Sumer, his wife, said it was a woman holding a baby. I turned it another way and said it was the group of angels that surround him. We each looked closely, moved it forward and back, turned it left and right, squinting to see it differently so that the lines would merge into one and we could see the clarity of the transitions of the lines and shadows and see the intended picture. Later in the evening, I held the picture in front of him and asked, "Would you explain the picture that you drew?"

To answer the question, he drew another picture; "What is this?" he asked. She said, "A chalice," then he set it on the table and turned it over, and she said, "A light house." I suggested perhaps a candle but conceded it could be a light house. He drew another picture and said, "What is this?" She thought a banana, I replied, "A sword." He leaned forward in his chair, his eyebrows furrowed and intent. He held his cigar in his right hand, between forefinger and thumb. He rolled it gently. With the index finger of his left hand, he gently tapped the drawings. Leaning forward and looking directly in my eyes, his gaze pierced my inner self. I felt vulnerable but safe. He broke into a small smile, and then like an instructor speaking to his protégé, in a deep and raspy voice, he began to speak. He addressed her and me, his words flowing gently but with a resolve that could only originate from within his heart.

> He: I did not have to tell you what these were, you saw and understood them as images from your memory and experiences. If I told you that this was "this" or "that," you would look at it, confused, because it would mean nothing to you. I drew something, and when I look at it, I see what I drew. What is interesting is that I listen to you, you describing what you see, and I enjoy what else is there. Why would I limit your thoughts or imagination by revealing what it is? You see me, smoking a cigar, my grandfather fishing, my grandmother playing an organ, or my mother sitting crocheting or carving. However, if you need a label to put on what you see here, then you may label this life; it is what you make of it.

Over this week at their home, we talked frequently and openly. There was so much to review. I talked to him about my conversation with his uncle. He thought of this, he meditated. He would drop into a spiritual state and talk to me at length. On this particular day, he once again looked me in the eye, puffing his cigar, that same furrowed brow and piercing eyes. He talked, he laughed, he teased my emotions. When I thought my questions would go unanswered, he would surprise me with instruction or an answer to a question presented earlier would arise from his heart. There he sat, me leaning back in my chair, sipping a cup of coffee, awaiting more information. Then:

He: When you speak with them you must understand that they do not have the catalyst that you have. For you there are only two options, and one of those options is unthinkable. Because of that catalyst, it is easy for you to move in the direction of belief. You experience, you hear, you weigh the information. It is either true, or it is not true. If the latter would be the case, then the unthinkable, the unacceptable must be acknowledged, that your son is hallucinating and insane. This catalyst pushes you easily to belief, but others do not share that view. They are not given the same set of criteria with which to evaluate the information. Yes, it is true, but those options do not include the evaluation of the information that is provided, its accuracy or its source. The two options do not consider the uniqueness of that information. From where did it originate? How could it know your thoughts, your questions posed in the middle of the night when no other person was around? No, those things are not considered, or for your mind do they need to be considered.

PATHS TAKEN

I travel back in time, within my thoughts, once again and repeat the incident nearly fourteen years ago when Mimi and I received a call from Sissy; Rich had been in an accident. Sissy did not know what had happened, only that he had been taken to the hospital. Mimi and I were at a work site, I told her we must go. She looked at me and said we were not finished; I just started throwing things in the car, repeating that we must go. I did not tell her what had occurred, waiting to hear more from Sissy, who was still making calls. She called again, he was at the emergency room of a local hospital, not far from us. Her mother, once again, asked what was happening, I told her that our son had been in an accident, I did not know anything more than that. We arrived at the emergency room, I was so scared I could hardly identify myself. The triage nurse told me that he was okay and led us to his room. He was sitting there, bruised and battered, his head hurting, his legs hurting. But he was okay, he smiled sheepishly. "Sorry Dad, Mom." He would later describe the moments before the head-on collision. Miraculously, he had no more than the apparent superficial injuries that we could see in front of us. We would not fully understand the depth of the injuries that occurred until much later. Many years later, we would get the full story, one bit at a time.

So much has occurred since then. Since that transitional day, we have engaged in daily phone calls and frequent trips to visit them, or they to visit us. Each contact is unique in and of itself, always something new presented. I often feel guilty about my expectations, each time he asks if it was worth it, the information that I receive, compared to the pain that wrenches his body as a part of that deliverance. The answer is always yes, the information I receive is worth it—so much so that I cannot hold it to myself alone; I must share it with you so that you may experience and understand the full depth of God's love and the pain that is experienced by those he sends to be the messengers, those who carry the message to you. Their willingness to undergo the pain, to deliver the message of God, the message of love. For them the pain is worth it, that you may understand the depth of God's love.

I walked into his living room; he was sitting quietly on the couch, relaxed, almost asleep. He began to talk, and I listened:

> He:[23] It was different that day, the hallway longer, darker. I saw him sitting there, in my room. An old man, plaid pants, flannel shirt. Sitting, looking at me. "Fighting with your sister again?" he asked. "Yes," I said. "It happens," he replied. Had I known then, what I know now, I would have been less anxious to befriend him, but how could I have known? He seemed so nice. He told me things and made me promises. I challenged his words, but he said he would provide proof. For each time he gave me something, I was to give something back to him. What did he want? He wanted my life. I told him that I could not give it to him, that my family loved me and it would hurt them too much. He told me that they hated me, and he could prove it. I did not think that this was possible, yet on that day, I heard the very words of hate from my own mother's lips. What

---

[23] Rich is talking, he is very relaxed, I did not think he was "in spirit" at the time, but I really was not sure.

I did not know then was the depth of his deception. He would show me things, but he would not explain the underlying pain and stress on my family that caused the overreactions. It was, however, on the day that my sister told my father that something was wrong and he must do something, on that day when he picked me up from my room with the help of one of my friends. He picked me up and took me to the hospital to save my life. It was on that day that the old man appeared as a friend for the last time. After that the pain and terror of his visits cannot be adequately described.

This was the first and really only time that he has opened up with an explanation of the events that followed the accident and the torment that followed. If I had fully understood, I doubt that I could have changed it, for even as I suspected it, nothing that I said or did really made a difference. What would happen was already in the works, the next step in the process was completely up to him. I gave him all the support that I could and continued my frequent conversations with Cyd. She continued to try to help me understand and help me keep him focused on the light.

I watch various television reality shows about paranormal activities, priestly exorcisms, chanting, crosses, and challenges to the negative energies, to show themselves, to rebuke them and cast them out. I can only tell you from what I understand, you do not have the power to accomplish what you would like to imagine, on the behalf of the victim. Only the victim may exercise choice, and that choice is to keep their focus on God, to practice daily positive energy exercises that breathe in the positive force of God and exhale the negative energy. It is not something that is accomplished overnight, over a week, or even a year. It is not something that may conclude at the end of even this lifetime. But do not give up, do not stop trying. When we take a moment for God, we in turn take a moment for ourselves. When we take that moment to appreciate God and feel his love, we in turn take a moment to appreciate ourselves and love ourselves. When we accomplish this, it is then that we can truly appreciate others and love others around us.

CHOICES

The morning walk was good for the dog and me. The temperature was around 39 degrees, and I was concerned with my wife catching cold before her trip to Maryland, so she stayed inside. I was also worried about my toe and did not know how far I could walk. I thought a mile or so. My mind was filled with thoughts, I wondered about the future for family and myself. I looked around me, where I was located, and hastened to the knoll at the edge of the golf course, where I could observe the morning sunrise. The stress rose as I realized that I would not make it in time, the sun would rise above the horizon, and I would miss that magical moment in my mind. It was an important moment; each morning I would go to that point and await the sunrise. Just at the moment, the birds would also rise, filling the morning sky as they left their perches and proceeded in flight to the west, where they would land and search for their morning meal in the grass, or land on rooftops and flutter about in the early morning warmth. These were good moments, and I began to worry that I would miss that feeling. Strange as it may seem, it also began something negative, the need to be at that point each morning. I was cautioned that the negative energies could even use the beauty of the morning to control me and what I do. I struggled to understand all that was occurring, I followed the conversations with Rich and engaged in multiple conversations with family, trying to explain to them what I had discovered, to share with them. Once again I was cautioned, "You are not the messenger," they told me. Instead, they said, "You are the listener, be comfortable as the listener, it too is an important role."

He:[24] You are like the person that stares at the sun and says, "Look at the light, look at the light." While the angel standing next to you says, "Why look at the light? Look instead at all it illuminates."

Me: I try to understand, to accept, but it escapes me.

He: Because you are deaf to the tones.

Me: (I thought a moment) How do I fix it?

He: It is not meant for you.

Me: (I interrupt) I will try . . .

He: You are . . . you . . . , think in terms of the parable.

> *A horse eating grass down the row, running, galloping in the field. Running free, beautifully, across the grass. As the horse runs it looks up into the sky and sees a bird soaring in the winds. Soaring, floating, riding the breezes. So free, so beautiful. The horse, seeing this, thinks, "I wish I were the bird, floating in the heavens, so blessed with this gift of flight, enjoying life so much more than I, fixed to the ground." Then the bird drops from the sky, landing on the grass in the field. It hops across the field on two feet, struggling through the tall grass, clumsily moving from place to place. The bird looks up and sees the horse galloping across the field, gliding effortlessly across the green meadow, wind blowing its mane, it tail flowing in the breeze it creates. So beautiful, so blessed; the bird looks on the sight enviously and says, "I wish I were the horse."*

He: Such are you, the horse in the field, blessed with who you are, but wishing you were the bird. Don't wish the life of another, instead rejoice in the life you have.

Me: I try to rejoice, but there are so many painful memories, negative thoughts that take control of my mind. I try to push them to one side and ignore them. Suppress those thoughts and memories that I may focus on what I have at this moment of time.

---

[24] Rich, "in spirit," state two.

He: Do not suppress those memories. They are a part of you. Embrace those memories that you try to throw away. Embrace them as bastard children, to be loved equally. Embrace them as you do the other memories that fill your mind, the good memories. Embrace them as the others such that they do not control you. As often is the case, like the pedophile that runs away to priesthood to find the answers from God, to hide in the church and think that because he is there in the church that these desires will be suppressed and disappear. But because the desires are hidden in the dark, they just become stronger and are then unleashed upon those who come to him for comfort and guidance. The beast grows in the dark, so do not keep him there. If you have an infectious wound, you do not think to hide it until it goes away. No, instead you give it attention to help it heal. To cleanse it daily, to apply antibiotics and clean dressing, to let it air, you help it to heal. Likewise, these negative things in your mind, give them attention to help them heal. Do not ignore them.

He: Accept who you are, give the time and energy to cleanse the wounds, do not wish to be the bird if you are the horse. If you are the horse, enjoy the life as the horse.

(I thought for a moment)

Me: I am not sure that I know how, how to embrace who I am and live as I am.

He: To say that you want to know all, to understand everything, suggest that you are in a hurry to die, to depart the world. Are you in a hurry to die?

Me: No, I am not in a hurry to die.

He: Then why must you know?

Me: To help the ones I love.

(There was a brief moment of silence, and then he spoke again.)

He: Do you think yourself the sacrificial lamb? That you would assume the burdens for all? Do you think that you alone receive this guidance and communication from God?

Me: Yes, I admit, I sometimes think that I am blessed more than others, given gifts that others do not receive.

He: The blessings that you receive, you receive because you ask for them. The blessings and messages are always there. They are there for everyone who desires to listen. Others do not hear because it is their choice not to do so. The tornado of thoughts, of questions, blaze through your mind. Be careful that this tornado does not destroy the farm that you have built. I spoke to you earlier from the parable of the lion and the gazelle. You are not different, cheering for the gazelle as it escapes from the lioness, but weakened by the sight of the starving cubs. You cannot have it both ways. To save the gazelle, the cubs must starve. To save the cubs, the gazelle must be sacrificed.

Me: I understand, I understand that I am weak, my mind filled with thoughts, challenged with the desire to know and understand.

He: God loves you and everyone around you, equally and with infinity. So simple, so simple.

METAMORPHISMS

He:[25] "Think in terms of a chain. A chain is as strong as it weakest link. Now consider a chain of three links. These three links are your links. The chain is the link from earth to heaven. The first link is your love of yourself. The second is your love for others. The third is your love of God. Unlike a chain of unequal links, one weaker than another, this chain is of equal strength for each link. We often overload one link, but for a balanced life, we must balance the load on each link."

Messages come in subtle ways, but we lose a lot in translation. I have been in multiple conversations and have received information, some that I share with you and some that I keep for myself, as those are not meant for you. There are times that I may overstep my boundaries and share information as if it were my job to be a messenger. I was asked if it was my desire to be a messenger. I think the question was rhetorical, as even I know that I do not have the courage to serve God in such a capacity. No, they explained to me, it is not my task, it is not my life. He explained to me, "You are the listener."

No, to be a messenger is not my job. I doubt that I could have the strength to forego all to be so honored. I accept the role of the listener, though not good at it. I will try harder and present to you what I have heard, as the listener, such that you can see what this experience has meant to me and that, from what I share, you may find something of value to your own life or spiritual evolution.

---

[25] Lessons from Rich, "in spirit," perhaps state one.

One morning in September of 2010, we walked about two miles, stopping for a moment, and then about this time I received a call from Sumer. She said that we had a visitor who wanted to talk with me:

She: Zophiel wishes to speak with you.

Me: I am here.

He: A thousand thoughts rage through your mind like a million raindrops on the surface of a still pond. The surface of the pond has become so disturbed that you can no longer see your reflection. You cannot see yourself because of those thoughts. Clear your mind so you will see who you are. Just be Richard. All you have to do is live your life and be yourself. You have many questions, you may ask.

Me: I know not what to ask you.

He: A thousand thoughts call me to the surface like air bubbles, yet when I arrive the questions are gone.

Me: I am humbled by your presence, I don't know what to ask.

He: Why only now?

Me: Yes, I guess you are always there.

He: You guess?

Me: (I spoke of something, but then made reference to listening) I try to be the listener, but I am not good at it.

He: You are a father, a brother, a son. You are a husband and an uncle. Are you perfect at being any of these?

Me: No, I do not think I am perfect at them, though I try my hardest to be the best I can.

He: Just because you are not perfect at them, doesn't change the fact that you are those as mentioned, as is with being a listener. You are the listener, keep trying.

Me: I had a dream, what did it mean? (Note to reader: I cannot remember all of the details, it was just one of many. In this dream I saw myself, along with others. I had something in my hand, it was a ticket or a check. There was a sum of twenty thousand dollars that I saw, perhaps more. It was confusing, as if I were to do something, but I was not sure what it was that I should do.)

He: An old dog had a dream. In the dream he was chasing a car and caught it. He awoke and looked at the angel beside him. The old dog said, "Does this mean that I will be able to run again?"

Me: I understand, it was just a dream.

He: You have so many questions on your mind. "What should I do today? What about this? What about that? Do I say this? What about tomorrow? Who was I then? When was my first life? How many times have I lived?" Clear your mind. The number of lives you have lived is not important, it is enough to know that it began with Nathaniel. Do not worry about your past lives, live the life you live now.

Me: Yes, I will try.

He: Know that God loves you. We all love you.

THE LOTTERY

It was August 26, 2009, two days before I was to purchase the lottery ticket. The Powerball lottery was at $41 million. I struggled to understand the gift and the path that I must follow. Not everything made sense, but each day I got up and walked. I started my fast as provided to me. I listened intently to the many messages that appeared in my thoughts; most were superficial.

Date: August 26, 2009[26]

I spoke extensively to Sissy about the issues of following the direction given to her. She stated that she had failed on multiple occasions. I asked her not to despair, that this was evolution

---

[26]   My notes.

not revolution. I told her that the mistakes were an important milestone, that they are important because she was beginning to think differently. She recognized her mistakes. For an example of the learning that had already occurred, I discussed with her the attempt to get to her appointments yesterday. Because of this task she was able to understand the need to return home. I spoke to her of the significance of the kidney stone and how something so small could make such a difference. I told her to think in terms of we and not I, in terms of giving and not receiving. I talked to her of examples, of her son and how he is teaching her to understand giving. I asked her to open her heart and to work extensively with her husband to understand that there are things that we can do, to compromise, as an example of . . . compromise, that was not the word I used, it was more like concessions, that we do not have to be right all the time, that sometimes we can concede. Sometimes we can help other people succeed as well, it does not always have to be our decision, our success.

I called Rich, he responded that he felt funny; there was a moment of silence and then a voice spoke.

He:[27] When stranded on an island do not look at a map to find the treasure, the treasure is useless on the island; instead look at the map to know where you are.

Me: Zophiel! I don't understand, would you clarify?

He: When stranded on an island do not look at a treasure map to find the treasure. The treasure is useless to you when alone on the island; instead look at the map to know where you are. To gain understanding (I was uncertain of this word), to know where you are on the island. It is a parable, seek meaning in the parable. The answer is there, very simple, very clear. The parable is for you. So many questions cloud your mind. So many questions. You may ask.

Me: I understand there is a path that I've taken and the decisions I've made are based upon the instructions I am given, and their association with Friday, August 28. The direction is clear, these are the Powerball instructions and there are the daily walks and the need to bring her closer from the physical to the spiritual. I

---

[27] Rich, "in spirit," state two. Conversation with he that watches over me.

accept and believe that this is the path that I must follow and that regardless of whether confirmation is chosen to be given, that I will follow that path because I believe it's the true path. If I were provided confirmation, it would help me.

He: The answer to the question is in the parable at the beginning of this message. There are so many questions. You may ask me two questions.

Me: Yes, there are many questions, and you know those questions. Please help me choose two of the questions that are most important to ask of you.

He: Yes, I know your questions, just choose two.

Me: Who is Elijah?

He: No one.

I am silent for several minutes. He prompted me for the question again. I sought the question I must ask in my mind. So many thoughts of choosing the right question.

Me: What is my true path?

He: You ask a question as though you don't know. You are on it. Why do you ask what you already know? If you wish to make your second question, again, one you know the answer to, okay.

The path you are on is the path you are supposed to be on, to love that which you love. You struggle, that is expected; you anticipate, that is good.

The suffering that you see is necessary, do not gaze on it as the treasure on the map. The answer is in the parable, find meaning in the parable and you will find meaning in the question.

Know that God loves you! So simple but so difficult to comprehend by so many. How could something so simple be so hard to see? But it is the nature of man, to make it difficult to understand.

Continue on the path you are on. You are not being misled. We care for you. We are all around you, we cheer for you. Open your ears, open your mind, open your heart and hear us.

That is the confirmation that you seek.

Why, I ask you, would we cheer if you were doing it wrong?

You struggle for your true name. Something so powerful is not meant for your ears yet. Otherwise, I would give it to you. Have patience. Follow the path given to you.

Consider the seven links. What is on the center link?

Me: The center link is blank.

He: Yes, what is on this center link? It is blank.

Me: I understand, I understand that the name will be given to me at the right time, and that name will be my true name.

At this point, the conversation was over. My son woke up, or more accurately he began the process of waking up. When he awoke, he stated, "We must have gone on a walkabout, my head in is killing me, and I am sick to my stomach."

He cleared his throat, he got a couple cups of coffee, and we spoke of the message. Sumer called him, and he linked us up together in the conversation. I told her of the message but stated we would discuss it later. I hung up to resume the work day.

August 28, I took the day off. On my morning walk, I thought about the message and the meaning of the parable. I prepared to go and buy the lottery ticket per my instructions. Still I hesitated. I thought about the meaning of the parable. It did not make sense to me that I should alter the lives of many by using God's gift in this way. How would the results affect the anchors that lock my life and the life of the ones I love to earth? My daughter's gift of medicine, would the money alter her life such that another life would be lost because she was no longer a doctor? And the path of my son, how would it be changed? My brothers' pride and arrogance, what changes would be made in their lives? How was it that I could assume this burden of change? To drive change against their will, it did not seem right. It was like God had given me another door to open, and all of his messengers were looking at me to see what I did. I made my decision. The gift that God was giving me was not intended to build treasure on earth. Instead, the gift was provided that I may understand where I am in relation to the spiritual connection to God. Knowing this, I will be better able to release my earthly anchors and prepare to return home when the time comes. But it may not be just about me, I struggle to share what I have discovered.

No, I did not buy a lottery ticket, I did not check the numbers, I have not checked the numbers I bought in July, and I have not bought any numbers since that day. Should God ever decide that this path is needed, then He will deliver the message without question, along with the instructions for its use. For now, I will think about the powerful journey that I am on, thinking not about the destination, but applying my energy and focus on the glory of that experience. So you then ask, "Why not check?" I say, "Why check?" If I check and the numbers are there, then do I spend my time questioning my decision not to buy the numbers? And if not there, then is it because I did not follow the direction to buy the numbers on August 28? What would that prove? The fact is, I have no doubt whatsoever of the outcome had I purchased the six numbers provided. That fact was a Powerball jackpot of $41 million was placed in front of me to choose if I desired. The choice presented was simple. Option 1: Select the money to build the treasure for this life. Option 2: Walk away from the earthly treasure and apply my energy to understanding where I am and where I should be going. Again, why is it important to speak of this to you? Is it an internal struggle with self, and therefore I bring this forward to seek your approval and acceptance? Do I want you to think of me in terms of some level of righteous glorification? It seems strange that I would even type those questions of self-doubt. But I must open all wounds, that they may be cleansed and healed, even the new wounds. In my mind, I am simply attempting to convey to you another simple message: "Where your treasure lies, so lies your heart."

This was not about money or personal wealth. The options presented were real, but the outcome was somewhat understood, even at the beginning. It is not about the physical, it is about spiritual growth.

You must separate the two, to truly understand. To grow spiritually does not restrict physical success; however, physical success can impact spiritual growth. I think about a phrase in the Book of Robes that says, "It is easier to lead a camel through the eye of a needle than for a rich man find his way to heaven." In this case, the eye of the needle is a mountain pass of very difficult but not impossible terrain (I only surmise this, as I have never been there). Still, from what I have received and understand, where your treasure lies, so lies your heart. If you have surrounded yourself with treasure here on earth, so will you be anchored to that treasure. "Anchored" is a metaphor for a binding to that which is here on earth. When you pass, you will be anxious to resume life here, with what you have, or you will find yourself suffering from another area of self that must also be addressed, and you continue working on the many branches of the tree that was planted so many lifetimes ago that you have lost completely the original problem you were hoping to resolve. For now, please accept what I mean, when I say it is not important about physical wealth or health, attending church, being a part of the congregation, or a pillar to the community, or a beggar on the street. God loves all equally. If you find success here, that is okay, but do not let it anchor you to this lifetime. What I received was an angelic numerical sequence, 8-2-8. It was presented in the form of a date in order for me to remember it. I received additional information that I could use to help me grow from one spiritual level to another. All of the information was important for me, as a person, as a child of God. If you look, you will not find the numbers here, I have not presented them to you, nor have I checked them. To see them there could only cause regret. That would not be something they desire for me to experience. It really does not matter. I chose the path I am on, because I desire to know where I am. I want to use the map to serve God, to grow spiritually and, with all of this, let what I have experienced help me attend my farm.

AN INTERPRETATION

[28]*He looks at this book and thinks of the Psalms of David. We get these messages and put them into the context of our lives. David received messages, thoughts, answers to his prayers. Consider Psalm 3, when he stated, "Oh Lord, how many are my foes, how many rise up against me. Many say to me that God will not rise up and be with us." It continues that the Lord gives deliverance and protects his people. If you look at this writing you can see the thoughts of David, of which he suffered. In the first verse, he is saying simply, "Save me, deliver me." So why is it that he says this, that God is the shield around me, the protection? That he bears a heavy load for all of those around him that depend on him, that he carries this load. He states that God looks down on him from the holy hill. He does not mean that God is standing on top of the mountain, but that although God is shouting the answer, he cannot hear it clearly, as if the words were coming from far away at the top of the mountain, that the words will come but when they come, they will be like a faint whisper.*

In verse 7 he says arise, deliver me, help me. In this he means that he is simply looking for God to assist him, to help him to see, and when he states for God to shatter the teeth, he is simply saying shatter the gnashing teeth of stubbornness and ignorance, to shatter the blindness to help them see the glory and love of God. He, David, was a man living in violent times, and the interpretations of the words are simply miscommunication of the message that is being given. That he is crying of the load he bears, to help the people to understand the love of God. David is surrounded by negative energies; he lies down and sleeps, and waits for the word. He seeks that everyone will receive the message to know what it is like to love and be loved. This is his turmoil.

When we look at these words, we can move back to our time, to our family, and create an analogy. These words that I share with them, that I hear, and they hear from me, they are not the first time these words

---

[28]   Lesson from Rich; I don't think he was "in spirit." He is just in a teaching mood.

have been spoken, they will not be the last. That when people hear these words, that they will gnash their teeth in blindness, that they would refuse to believe, but if they were to put the words into beliefs, imagine how much more could be accomplished.

> [29]*You read in the Bible of God smashing a man of wickedness to oblivion, that you would see that God would crush the man and cast him into hell. But again, we miss the story and meaning. What was seen was blackness, that the blue becomes blackness and then when he looks he sees the blackness no more. Therefore the man was destroyed. But this is not the case, that when you take a person of anger, of wickedness, that when this person's mind and heart are opened to the beauty of God's love, that when he sees this, he will say that he too wants to love in that same manner. And at that point, all that lives in this person is goodness, love, good will. The wickedness is gone, it is "smashed into oblivion." The blackness is replaced with the white light of God. The soul lives on, in the light of God. This soul that lives in infinity, this line that is never ending, would you imagine that God would destroy that soul, when it has time immortal to find its way home? It is not destruction of the soul that occurs, but simply the banishment of darkness, of negative energy. Even though David wrote of the violence, there was not one act of violence that occurred. Instead, the only thing that occurred was the banishment of hate, replaced with love. If you truly could understand his thoughts, what he was feeling, then you could surely see how these passages were simply lost in translations.*

The angelic sequence, 8-2-8, a transition, the metamorphosis of the human soul. From flesh to spirit, from spirit to flesh. For such a long time, I have thought about the purpose of the butterfly. Why did God put such a beautiful creature on the earth for us to behold? I thought of the caterpillar, breaking out of its embryonic state and then crawling about on the tree, eating leaves as fast as it can. Growing fat and plump, and then one day, weaving a cocoon about itself and going to sleep. No, not going to sleep but going through a metamorphosis, as one day the cocoon will open and from it emerge the beautiful butterfly. Look at this creature and behold the beauty of God's hand. The hand that would create such a wonderful transition, why would

---

[29] Continuation of the lesson above.

that transition be greater than our own, for us that are made in his image? I cannot find the verse within the Book of Robes that describes that God created the butterfly in his image. So why the butterfly? I ask this in a rhetorical sense, but honestly I think that the butterfly exists for our understanding. That we could look upon this beautiful creation and recognize what is possible for us. We exist, that is true; after all, we can see ourselves and others around us. We can feel, hear, smell, taste, think, and act upon our thoughts. Yes, as Descartes stated, "I think and therefore I am." We exist.

What we don't know is what we cannot see, or touch, or feel, or smell, or hear, or act upon. Some of us might consider that if we are unable to check off these boxes, that it does not exist. In ancient times, such thoughts appear to be prevalent, as what one was able to see was very limited, and therefore existence was very small. Yes, we know of people of vision who were able to see and tell us of what they saw. Some documented their visions within the Book of Robes, the chapter called the Revelation of John is an example. When we look at the words written, I fall back to my earlier discussion on learning by reference. In this case, we observe John seeing things that he could only describe in the terms of his understanding. He spoke of giant fire-breathing insects and other things in the context of his knowledge base. When we look at these descriptions today, we do not really understand what he saw but can only interpret what we think he saw.

The same is true for other chapters or books from the Book of Robes. We don't really know what actually happened, or the real intent of the author, but what we do know is the overall approach to the book. That approach, the approach that I understand, is to provide some information of historical significance, some fictional stories or examples, and some information that is lost in understanding, such as parables. But why parables? The answer is in the Book of Robes. It is discussed in the New Testament, when the disciples asked Jesus why he spoke in parables. He replied that it was presented in a way that would be understood by those who truly sought to understand. I find it amazing that there exist a set of books that have been so read and studied that the books themselves have become, to some, more important than God. All that was said is converted to what is understood, but who is to say that what is understood today is the same as what was said then? Of greater curiosity, why are words that were spoken so many years ago more important than words spoken today? Is the answer that many have stopped listening, preferring instead to struggle with interpretation of that which is no longer applicable?

I don't mean to dismay you or let you think anything wrong about this, but to ask you to consider what you read and understand its meaning. Understand its meaning, and you may understand God's love better. I don't want to suggest too much about what you do or do not understand; that would be arrogance on my part, so let me state that for myself, as I look at the words today, I can look on them with a different understanding. My path is a simple path. I must care for my farm. While I go about caring for my farm, I seek to gain knowledge, and where knowledge is not permitted, I seek understanding, and where understanding does not come, I ask God to help me with patience, that I have patience with myself and given that patience that I will better understand myself. Given a greater understanding of myself, that I can learn to love myself. And then, with a love of self, I can then learn to love others.

There is a lot of "givens" presented here. To explain, we are all made in the same essence of God, and because we are all of the same essence, that love of self is essential for us to love others, that are also made in that same essence. If we love ourselves and others, then we can form a stronger bond with our love of God and hence connect the three links of our chain. That is what I desire, to balance the three links of the chain: self, others, and God.

ANOTHER DREAM

One week ago, I awoke from a dream. Perhaps it was frightful, perhaps it should have been. Honestly I don't remember being scared or worried. But I was concerned about the dream, as I had seen myself die in a car accident. I was not the driver of the car, I was a passenger. There were people looking at the scene of the accident, I was watching and listening to what they were saying. As they spoke, I could see the playback of the events as they unfurled. It was confusing. There was a DVD player in the car, and I was trying to put a DVD into the player that was located in the dash. The DVD would not fit into the player, as it was broken in four places. I struggled to insert the DVD but was distracted as the car was going fast and approaching a corner, or the end of the road, perhaps a T intersection. I can recall a grass bank. I can also recall reaching down and trying to loosen the gas pedal, which was stuck. The people were talking, they said that although I was wearing a seat belt, the belt did not lock itself at the point of the impact. This was because the DVD was not working. There was a connection between the DVD player and the inability of the seat belt to work. Things were not aligned, and it meant that I was not being protected, and therefore I died in the accident.

I talked to my son about this dream, he listened as I described the events I remembered. It was a short conversation, we passed back and forth our love and then went on about our day. The next day, he called and we discussed the possible message that I received.

To understand the dream, we must dissect the components of the dream and then interpret the relationship of that component to myself. Component number 1 is the driver of the car. Of interest was the fact that I am not the driver, and therefore I am under the control of someone else. The second component is that the driver may have been a work associate. He is certain that I said so in my first description of the dream to him, so I accept that as true. After a week, I could not recall that person's face or identity. The next component is the broken DVD. Clearly the DVD is broken, and it does not matter if the DVD is inserted into the player or not, it will not function. So why the stubborn push to load a broken DVD? Next, the accelerator is stuck and the car is speeding down the road toward a definite end. There is no time to fix it or stop what is happening, but I still try to do so. Then the seat belt; I was wearing the seat belt, which is not my normal habit. But the seat belt does not function as intended. Though I consider myself safely secured, I am not. Lastly, the observations of those who looked upon the scene and describe why the seat belt failed.

The interpretation of the dream was that I was on a path where I have given up control and where I am allowing distractions that are superfluous; if not corrected, these distractions could result in catastrophic events. Then, there was the seat belt, where I feel that I am secure in my environment, but that could be misleading. The direction was to look closely at all that is occurring around me, remove the distractions, clear my mind, and not rely on superficial things that may seem secure, but will offer no protection when that protection is necessary. Consider all things, work life balance, family, associates, my own health. Take control of my life, do not put that control on others, to give up on life and live to work. Balance of life is hard to achieve, there are many perceived obstacles, some that I create on my own, yet I put the burden of that control on others. I have the choice to stop eating when I am full. I do not need to eat all that is placed before me, just because it is there. It is my choice to accept the call to work all hours of the day. To put family equal or above work is important. There must be a balance to life. My life is unbalanced, that was the message of the dream. My life is unbalanced, and I need to change it, to find balance.

KNOW THEY ARE WITH ME ALWAYS

One day, I was on my morning walk, with Bailey. We had nearly completed the four-mile route and were nearing the final turn to home. I looked at the easterly morning sky, the beams of sunlight bouncing off the clouds suspended there. The colors were glorious. The morning was crisp, the temperature around 32 degrees, the air fresh. I held my head up and straightened my back. Gazing to the east, I asked God for courage and understanding. I asked God to help me to understand myself, that I may learn to love more. It has been a few weeks since last I spoke to his messengers, and I was feeling alone. I struggled to deflect the negative energies that crawled upon my shoulders and dug into the flesh of my back. I know they are there, I know what they would drive me to think and say. I wish them gone, but they linger on. My messages have been clear, to overcome them I must just continue what I do each and every day. Focus on the positive energies of God, give God his time. Try and try again.

On this morning, I tried to focus on this latter approach, to give to God his time and to seek understanding of self, that I may learn to love more. We turned left at the road, the final quarter mile to the house. We were now off the avenue and into the residential area. We approached the Y in the road and swung left toward home. As we passed that intersection, half way to the house, all of a sudden I heard two honks at my side. I looked quickly to my right and there, passing me, barely above my head and gliding down the middle of the street, were two Canada geese. Past me, they soared majestically and then they swooped up in a massive arc and floated over the top of the house to my front. I watched them in their glorious flight until they passed out of sight, stopped there on the sidewalk, gazing intently at what had just happened. Coincidence, perhaps, but not for me, no; for me this was a simple sign from those who watch over me to let me know that I am not alone. They are always there, helping, listening. All I need to do is open my heart, open my mind, open my ears, and listen.

August 31, 2009[30]

I got up early, 5:00 a.m. as usual. By 5:15 a.m. Bailey and I were on the street taking our normal morning walk. We walked toward Safeway and passed Pace, turning left into the Kings Sooper parking lot. We crossed Pace again and entered the Safeway parking lot. We walked across the parking lot and then returned to the sidewalk on 17th. I was worried about the time. I needed to extend the walk in order to arrive at the end of the golf course at the time of sunrise. I considered alternate paths. When the thought came to me:

Do not put a crown on God's head.

Do not create an altar.

Return home, clean up, and go to work.

September 1, 2009

I got up early, 5:00 a.m. as usual. By 5:15 a.m. Bailey and I were on the street taking our normal morning walk. We proceeded down the same path as taken the day before. This time as returning along 17th, the thought came to my head:

---

[30]   My personal notes.

Jesus did not preach in the temple, he always spoke to the people in the open, in a field. He tried to teach them in accordance to their understanding; that they believed themselves a sinful people and that they believed that they must be cruel to each other and offer sacrifices to redeem their sins. He therefore told them that their way to heaven was through his way; that he is the path; that they did not honor God, but honored their faith and that the ritual of their faith was more important than the honor to God.

I completed my walk, stopping a few moments in the golf course to observe the sunrise. The sunrise was masked by fog. After the time of sunrise, we began the journey to the house. En route, a large flock of birds flew over our heads. I rejoiced in the gifts that God has bestowed upon me.

After cleanup and breakfast, I called my daughter and spoke to her briefly about the morning and asked how her mother was doing. After a few minutes, we completed our conversation, and I called my son. I spoke to him about the thoughts of Jesus. He shared my thoughts and spoke about the time of crucifixion and the destruction of the temple.

October 14, 2009

Rich called me about 4:35 p.m. He stated that he had a message for his sister. I said, have you given her the message yet? He replied that he had not. He did not want to bother her at work. I stated that she was home at this time and said he should call. He asked me to call and add her into the conversation. I asked what the message was, he stated that she needed to buy new shoes. We discussed the meaning of this answer, then I called her and added her into the telephone conference.

He gave her the message, which she completely understood.[31] She was complaining about her toe, it was numb. She had been to a podiatrist to discuss the toe and it was not clear the reason. She worried of brain cancer, possible spine injury during birth of the children, or possible nerve damage from the C sections. He told her it was none of this and went into a detailed medical

---

[31] Rich was "in spirit," I think it was state two, I am certain later that it is Zophiel who I am talking to, but it may have been someone else earlier.

discussion that clearly she understood, but I could not follow. Then he told her just to buy new shoes.

We talked a few minutes longer, my son and I, after she disconnected from the phone call, and then there was a change, a new voice who stated, "You have questions."

I did not ask who was addressing me, I understood.

Me: Yes, I have questions.

He: You may ask me two. Take your time to ensure they are the questions of which you want an answer to.

Me: No, I know the questions.

Me: What is happening to/with him? Please address this in terms of his home, his family, his physical life.

He: Your love is beautiful, your care is beautiful, your worry is sincere. If you must know, then know this, he will fall. All that he was, all that he would have been is a memory in imagination. Imagination of what he would have liked, desired, thought must be for him, but is not. Fall, he will fall into a life of that which is his to recover, from those of which he is to save. All those, those who will soon become his peers, his friends, to that which he is to save one more time. Will he like this? No. Will he enjoy this? No. Will those who love him enjoy watching him do this? No. Will his wife stand by him in this? That is her choice to do so. Thus far, is yes.

He will sink farther than you in your life can possibly watch him drop, and it will hurt you to see him suffer. But despite this, all that you must endure and suffer, know that he is loved by all that is and ever was, and that which is greater than family.

Dear, dear Richard, father of that which he named as himself, he is loved and protected. This life is only an instrument of that which he loves and cares for. Worry not, for the suffering you see is only physical, because in the spiritual, he has all others would desire to achieve, and all that love him and care for him will share this love. In the spiritual world, he has all that anyone could wish to achieve.

FROM FLESH TO SPIRIT

It was a Friday morning, I walked my usual path. On this morning, I called my mother to see how she felt; my aunt was there fixing her hair. We spoke briefly of my aunt's upcoming sermon. She said she was going to talk about the passage of the Bible regarding Jacob and his wrestling with the angel. I told her she should not take this passage in its literal connotation. Jacob did not put the angel in a headlock. I said that, if the angel had touched him, or if he had touched the angel, the overwhelming love that he would have felt would have prevented any thoughts of combat; he would have fallen to the ground and cried, feeling the awesome power of God's love.

As I walked on, many thoughts traveled through my head. These thoughts are not unusual; they are typical of my daily routine. As memories returned, memories that I thought I had suppressed, memories that I desired to suppress, I remembered the angel's words, *"Do not hide negative memories, instead cleanse them, as you would a wound."* At this point I was perhaps three miles into my walk. I gazed at the heavens; I prayed for assistance, that God would help me, that he would scrape away the rotten flesh, that he would lay maggots on the wound so that they would eat away the rotten flesh and cleanse the wound. I gazed longingly at the morning sky, hearing the normal sounds of cars. I was suddenly interrupted by a "pop," the sound like a bursting tire, a blowout. The screech of tires followed then and there, the arrival of rumbling, tumbling, the crashing sounds like a dump truck partially filled with large rocks and the sound of those rocks being thrown around in the bed of the truck as it went across a rut-filled road, bouncing and jostling its contents. I saw dust rising across the way, then silence for a moment, followed by painful screams in the morning stillness.

I struggled through my coat to find my cell phone and finally called 911. I hung up and proceeded to the crash site. Bailey and I approached the crash site; cars were stopped and other people had emerged from their homes, rushing to the aid of the victims of this tragic accident. A small boy was screaming and was being comforted by a gentleman as he cried for his father. I then saw his father being helped by another; he had a head wound but was alive and conscious. This man's car, bent and destroyed, was sitting on the edge of the road.

I then saw a more tragic scene, a light truck or SUV, its cab crushed, crumpled, completely destroyed. Next to the vehicle, a seat belt draped around a lifeless form, the facedown body of a small woman or child, I could not tell. I noticed the small shoes of the body as it lay there crumpled, I could not see the face, the clothes did not tell the story. Then a couple of feet away, laying on the ground, another person, face down, a man, the driver of the vehicle no doubt, but how he had gotten to this position was hard to imagine. It looked as if he had been thrown from the vehicle and in his last moments had tried to crawl to the other passenger's side. A gentleman was kneeling by the side of the man, feeling his neck; he looked up and stated there was no pulse.

A police car arrived; the officer got out of his vehicle and spoke briefly with the gentleman, acknowledged there were no survivors, and proceeded to the other vehicle. I stood there, wondering what I could do. Should I kneel down next to the victims and pray, should I call for the Angel of Mercy to bring them back, would it make a difference if I tried? I wondered if I should secure my dog to a fence and go help them, there on the sidewalk. I walked slightly away, tears flowed from my eyes, I looked up and asked that God's angels assist these two on their way home. After standing there for a moment longer, I walked back in the direction of the first vehicle and watched as others tended the injured.

An ambulance now arrived, and paramedics started treating the boy and his father. The man assisting the child turned and said to a woman, "I am coming back to the house, tell the children that though I am covered with blood, it is not mine, do not worry." I stood there, away from the activity, and again thought of what to do; another man approached and asked me if I saw what happened. He stated that he had heard the crash and had called 911. I told him I only heard it myself. At that point, another police officer arrived and asked the same question of me, my response was the same; tears were still running down my cheek. I stood there a moment longer and then turned toward the house and walked home.

After cleaning up and completing my morning rituals, I opened the garage door to go to work. A funny noise greeted me, like the sound of the car seat moving. Strange, I thought. My work that day was mostly uneventful. I returned home, and once again, as I walked through the garage, I heard this funny noise.

The next morning was my typical routine: I awoke, took my walk, and once again as I entered the house, I thought I heard something, like a voice or movement upstairs. I brushed it off and went to work. On this day, because it was nice outside, I put my hound dog out to spend the day. At about six in the evening, I returned home, and as I entered the house, I once again heard something funny. I went to the patio door, and upon opening the door, my dog rushed in. Whining, her nose to the floor, she ran frantically around the room and then darted up the stairs. This was so strange of her; I had not seen this before. I suspected that she had seen someone; thinking they may still be here, I cautiously proceeded up the stairs to see what was there. She ran through each room and then back down, stopping at her bed. Thinking that someone had been in the house, I checked each window and door but they were still secure. I found no evidence of anyone entering forcibly into the house. I went to bed that night, somewhat apprehensive. I was certain someone had been here and was considering the possibility of a spirit. The next morning, after my walk, as I entered the house, once again I heard a voice upstairs. This time as I walked across the room, I remembered what Cyd had asked for the young girl, and then I asked that Gabriel come to help the lost soul find their way home. There were no more sounds; Bailey did not search the house again after that request.

A couple of days later, Rich and Sumer called. He stated that they had a visitor at their house. They were sitting at the table on their screened-in patio, and while sitting there, they saw the locked screen door to the outside just open and close as if someone had walked through. They both acknowledged to each other what they saw; she went and checked the door, it was locked. Strange noises continued, and then they saw a tapestry hanging on the wall wave as if blown by a wind. There was no wind. Rich thought he felt something, an energy moving. As they told me about this, he got up and left the patio, going into the house. I asked Sumer what was happening, and she said he was talking to someone. He came back and summarized what had occurred.

It was explained to me that the spirit in the house was the spirit of the father who passed at the crash I had observed. This spirit had seen the positive energy that surrounded me and had followed me home, seeking assistance. The man's son had been killed in the crash, but the boy did not know he was dead and was lost between levels. The boy's father needed someone to talk to the boy and let him know what had happened. He, the father, could not go home without his son. My son said that he could help and asked me when he would be coming to Colorado again. I stated that he generally came in March. I said that if he wanted, I could buy him a plane ticket, but to get him here quickly would be expensive. He stated, "You would do this?" I replied, "Yes, if he wanted, I would do this."

He went off to speak to the spirit again and came back and said that he was told we could get a round-trip ticket for $161. After a bit more discussion, I went online and purchased the tickets, although they were more like $180. (During the course of the flight, my son received a couple of complementary gifts from the airline; after subtracting their value from the price of the tickets, the final cost was $161.) The final arrangements were made; on Saturday, November 21, at 3:15 p.m., my son would meet the spirit at the crash site.

On November 21, at three o'clock, we started walking toward the crash site. We did not know what to expect, but we were aware that Rich often needed assistance to move into a spiritual state; typically this was in the form of a small drink or cigar to help him relax. He refused both, stating it was not necessary. We walked the half mile to the site, and upon arrival he immediately took a seat on the ground. The temperature was about 54 degrees, the sun was shining. As he sat, he folded his hands beneath his abdomen and began to meditate. Each of us sat down on the ground a little away from him and waited. I closed my eyes and prayed for God to assist him in finding the boy. We sat there nearly twenty minutes as he meditated. Mimi and Sumer chatted quietly and I just listened and watched.

All of a sudden, he called Sumer to his side, and she helped him remove his coat, shirt, and undershirt. He resumed his position in meditation, stripped from the waist up. We waited another few minutes, and when my leg began to hurt, I stood up. I silently gazed around me, now about thirty minutes into the vigil, when a bird swooped down over the site, past me, calling, then swooping up in a steep arc, soaring up, circling, and then landing atop a light pole to our side. All the while the bird called, three to four times. I did not recognize the bird species, nor did I recognize its call, but that is not unusual as I am not an avid bird watcher.

There was a brief interlude, and Rich stirred, looked at us, and said it was done, it was time to go home. He stood and walked over to us. Sumer handed him his undershirt. As he started to put it on, he staggered for a moment and then sagged into her arms. I stepped up to help her hold him steady; he struggled for a moment, took a deep breath, and then raised up straight and continued to dress. She asked him how it went, and he stated he had found the boy. The boy naturally did not know him and was cautious, asking him who he was. He stated that he was from God and was there to assist. The boy asked why, if he was from God, he had all the protection. He told the boy that if that worried him, he would remove the protection, and that was when he undressed from the waist up.

At this point, sitting in the chilling afternoon air, he told the boy to look at him, bare from the waist up, sitting on the ground, sweat running down his brow. He said, behold the energy of all those around him, that energy being the warmth that would cause his body, bare from the waist up, to perspire in the chilling wind. He said that if that was proof enough, that he should open his eyes and see all those around him that were there to take him home, including his father and many of God's angels. It was at this moment that the boy opened his eyes and saw everyone around him and went to them. It was also at that same moment the bird swooped down, calling. The bird was not needed for the boy, or for anyone else, it was there for me, that I needed confirmation that something had occurred.

Rich had spoken to Cyd about this event; Sumer asked him whether Cyd was there, and he stated that she may have been, there was a lot of energy there, but he had not recognized her. Later in the evening, he searched the Internet for bird sounds and matched the sound to what everyone had heard. He played the sound for me, and I stated that it was the sound I heard. He then opened the picture of the bird, and it matched the one I had seen swoop down and land on the light pole. The bird was a northern flicker. At this time of the year, it is not common to see this bird. As I recall all of this, I think about the times I walked past the location of the accident, feeling the strange presence of something there, the pain of loss. However, after that afternoon with Rich and family, sitting there watching him meditate followed by the swooping bird, since that moment, it is just another place, a place of normal energies.

It is the Wednesday before Thanksgiving; we arrived in Florida last night. It was a quiet evening with family. After dinner, we retired to the porch; Rich lit a cigar, and we poured ourselves a good hefty scotch. It was a great eighteen-year-old sherry oak single malt, the pairing with the cigar was extraordinary. Although I do drink scotch, I quit smoking in 1991 and have never smoked since, so I have to take his word about the pairing. In any case, we reviewed the progress on this book. As the night came to a close, we talked about the upcoming morning walk, then I went to bed.

I was up at six o'clock, getting ready for my walk. Early in the morning, Mimi stated that she wanted to walk with me; however, she was sleeping soundly and I did not know the area or the quality of the path. At this point, it was better that she stay home, and I went out the door alone. It was a beautiful morning, crisp and moist. I did not think of much for the first half hour, just the path. I walked along the edge of the road, and finally, after some distance, I came upon a sidewalk, where I could now walk and think.

It was along the return path that it came to me, the thoughts of the Bible and its purpose. These thoughts were somewhat complicated, but my mind went back to a picture of the Star of David that was drawn just a few days earlier. I pondered the information that came to my mind, pondered it as well as a billboard I had seen earlier, no, not a spiritual sign, but a religious sign, a replica of him on the cross and the words "TORO HICE, POR TI" or "For you I give everything." My mind drifted, gently floated in the morning breeze. I had walked over two miles; somewhere on the third mile, thoughts pulled me toward the Bible, this book, what was it? Answer: "A lesson in history." A history lesson on what was, and then a lesson on what could be.

I sit now writing these words, trying to understand that which I have felt, those simple and complete words on the billboard. Superficial thoughts, or a message? I pondered its truth, and his words, the last words of Jesus, spoken on the cross, as quoted to me, quoted to me when I asked about them, those words. It is so amazing, amazing as time does not exist on the other side, one second here or five thousand years are all the same. When they gave me the answer, the answer did not seem like they were recalling the information, but that they were giving the words to me as they occurred. That they were looking upon the scene, seeing the tortured and brutalized body of him on the cross, white bones seen through ripped flesh, his weight bearing down on the nails that pierced his wrist, holding him to the cross. Tortured, shamed, humiliated, his blood flowing onto the ground, surrounded by angry mobs, mobs filled with hatred. He looked upon his captors, his torturers, those who mocked him, those who threw garbage at him; he looked down from the cross and said to them, "For all of you that look upon me with hatred, anger, and disgust . . . I love you all." His very last words, the last words spoken that day, from human form, on the cross: "I love you all."

My aunt had challenged the words that I gave her, she challenged the messages. My brother called me insane; my cousin said I was of the devil. "Oh my," I said to my aunt, "if you were standing there, on that day, looking, hearing him speak, would you have been one that demanded his crucifixion? What is it to which you cling so tightly; your religious belief and its book? Have you forgotten him, have you created something that you put above God?"

She admitted that she most probably would have been one of the many condemning him. Her main issue now is about physic communication and communication with spirits or nonphysical beings. My aunt quoted to me from the Old Testament, Deuteronomy 18, verses 9–13. She said, "What of these words, clear statements that those that communicate with the dead, those are despised by God?"

I said she misunderstood what was spoken, but alas, my understanding was weak, so I asked for information about these verses, and the answer was given to me:

> *He:[32] Why do you look upon that part of the book? That part is obsolete; it was rewritten by him, when he was here. All that was, was replaced. Why do you look at this and choose to pull up a single verse, pick and choose? If you were to follow that direction, then I suppose you would have to follow all of the direction, not just pick and choose what is convenient. But if you look at the entire chapter then you will see that the people were afraid, that Moses had just returned from the mountain and that although he had been in God's presence for just a couple of minutes, he had aged forty years. The people were afraid; they were afraid what would happen to them if God spoke directly to each of them. So they sought messages from others, from those who could communicate across the spiritual boundaries. But God said to them, in this land there are many that choose to go separate from me, that sacrifice their sons and daughters, that worship the negative energies; do not follow in their path, instead, because you want to know, I will choose from your brothers, one of you, to be my messenger and deliver messages from me to you. You will know they are from me when what they speak comes true."*

---

[32]   Rich, "in spirit," state two.

Within this explanation, they did not say that all information passed from people proclaiming physic abilities is pure. What was stated is that because the people want to know, that he would provide the capability of knowing from those among them, and that they would know they were of God when they spoke the truth. Here is the interesting point: the truth is often unknown by ourselves. Even when we hear it, we doubt its validity.

I reflect back on the continuation of my morning walk, thinking, pondering the information that has come to my mind. So many thoughts, so many questions; I arrived at the house and looked at my watch. It had been less than that required for a four-mile walk. I thought of my wife's request to walk with me and went to the door to see if she wanted to walk the next mile with me. She had just come from her morning shower and did not look ready for a walk. That was okay; I would just proceed on my own.

I walked around the bend and up onto a circle. At the top of the hill, a gated access road went to the left and led to another housing area. I looked at the gate, bent and sagging on its hinges. It appeared to have been rammed by a vehicle, but stayed there still. There were chains binding the two halves of the gate together and a bicycle lock at the base. It appeared that someone wanted this gate closed. I thought how nice it would be to go across, into another neighborhood, to find another path to walk. Instead, because of the barrier, I retraced my steps, back to the street. I could turn left and walk around the circle or retrace my steps to the right. I chose left but had just taken a couple of steps when a bird swooped down across my path and flew past me, calling loudly. I turned and watched the bird awhile. It was calling as it soared up steeply into the morning sky, circled, and then landed on a tall tree. I listened intently to its calls; I looked at it in the tree top, perched there, calling out occasionally, the calls so familiar in my memory. I walked toward it to get a better look; it glanced in my direction, and then, calling loudly, it swooped up from the tree and once again took flight into the morning sky. I watched it for a couple of moments as it sped away, making a huge circle and then turning and disappearing in the distance. Why was this bird such an interest to me? I often see birds, some in pairs, occasionally single birds, and in Colorado, huge flocks.

Why then the importance of this bird? It is simple, you see, it was the same bird I saw last Saturday. No, not the exact bird, I could not possibly know if that were the case, but the same species, a northern flicker.

I just completed reading this section to my son. Interestingly, but not unpredictably, he asked, "How did you feel?" He often asks that question when I recount an experience. Why, what is important about the feeling at that moment? I have asked him about this several times, enough to the point that I understand the answer, the answer which is another set of questions. Did you feel scared, apprehensive, warm, comfortable? What were the emotions at the time of this experience? Here I am now, weeks later, reading this section, making editorial changes. I did not answer the question when I wrote the paragraph. I am now sitting on a jet plane, returning from a holiday visit with family. I know the answer to the question, as I feel the same now as I felt then. I feel warm, comfortable, relaxed. That was my answer then, that is my answer now.

He listened to what I said, and then he just got up from the table and said he had a pang, something just hit him. What? Direction: take a drink, sit back, and meditate. Find the voice.

IN GOD'S SERVICE

I spoke with my daughter this morning and talked to her about the messages and information that had been provided. I recounted the events from the day before, and the task that has been offered to us, a task that came as a response to our request.

If we consider the task that God has passed to us, at our soul-level request, tasks that answer our plea for guidance and help, we must be prepared to receive and act on the answer provided, or else why ask for something that we do not want? That he answers our request and would give us a task to help us to achieve the goals of our request, and that we would choose to follow the direction of that task, and its rule set, is our choice. On the morning of July 30, 2009, I woke to bodily pains as usual, caused by my morbid obesity, and lumbered into the bathroom to take my morning shower. As I stood there with the warm water beating down over me, I pleaded for assistance. I asked God to help me shed this painful burden from my body, and on July 31, 2009, he gave me a rule set to follow.

> *Direction July 31, 2009*
>
> *On this morning I called Rich and we began a normal morning conversation. He states he is tired and immediately falls asleep.*
>
> *He:*[33] *Richard, Richard.*
>
> *Me: Yes.*
>
> *He: Richard.*

---

[33] Rich, "in spirit," state two.

Me: Yes, Zophiel? I am here.

He: Richard, you will get a piece of bass wood, 2 × 2 × 13. From this, you will create a wood chain of 7 links. Each link 1.5 × 2.5 with 0.5" diameter. The links are to be carved by hand and blade alone. Do you understand?

Me: Yes.

He: On the links, you will carve the names of those closest to you on each link, six names, three right and three left. The middle link will be left blank. Do you understand?

Me: Yes.

He: This will be gifted to your daughter. This will take priority over nothing, to be done during spare time, idleness only. This takes precedence over nothing save idleness. During the creation of the chain, protect the essence of the wood. Each link shall indicate or embrace the love of family.

You will fast, from the time the blade first touches the wood, until the last name is carved. You will consume calories during this time of 4, 2, 5, 2, 3, 2 every 2 hours in 100s, and no other time. 400, 200, 500, 200, 300, 200. Only during those times and no other time, do you understand?[34]

Me: Yes.

He: Three times during the fast you shall eat of the fruits of the earth, savoring their sweetness. Do you understand?

Me: Yes.

---

[34] This fast was given to me by them, it is not something that you should try to imitate, it was not meant for me to share with you as a method of weight control that others should practice. This is my fast, given to me alone, as stated in the directions. If you desire something like this, then you should consult your medical advisor or dietician. Other than that, if you open the door to receive their messages, perhaps you can receive their direction. Please understand, the words above are not superficial thoughts, words that came to my head or that I created. They were direct words spoken and heard clearly.

He: This message is for you and you alone.

He ended the conversation as quickly as it started, closing with "God loves you." I thought about the message and the task laid before me. How was I to accomplish this task? Rich awoke and asked me what had occurred. I did not reveal much, per what I had understood of the direction. We said our good-byes, and I proceeded with my work day.

Rich called later while he was driving to work. He stated that he had received a strange message to pass to me, the message was that the purpose was only for me and me alone. Did that mean anything to me? I said it did and then told him about the task.

On the first of August, I weighed in at 348 pounds. Three months later, I found myself at 297 pounds, the least I had weighed in fourteen years. Then on March 26, 251.5 pounds, a 96-pound drop in weight; August 14, 2010, 217 pounds; and March 2011, 192 pounds and still dropping. I have achieved that result from the blessings that God has bestowed upon me. I hold true to the task, the fast, that was given to me because it is what I want to do; it is my choice. God does not direct our actions, he does not tell us that we must do one thing or another; he has given us free will. We are free to decide what we will do or will not do; the freedom of choice is a gift from God. Whatever our decision, he will not love us less for that decision, nor will he love us more. God loves us unconditionally, a concept that is so simple but so difficult for us to understand.

I heard that Sissy was given information on positive energy exercises. She should find a place each morning and she should meditate a moment, just a moment, to absorb God's energy, a moment to rejoice in the life that God has given her, to hear the sounds of nature, of God's gifts to man. I heard that she went to a place of positive energy and sat there for three hours. I then understood that she did not return to the spot again, nor did she take additional time to mediate; she did not have time to spend on this effort. She was then given a challenge to not speak harshly to anyone, to not harm a thing, not even a spider, for thirty consecutive days, that should she fail on any day, that she must restart at zero. After many days, she reported that she would fail time and again, continually resetting her days back to zero.

When I thought about this, I considered it a travesty. This seemed such a simple task in my view, why could she not complete this task quickly and easily? What a surprise that I was given the same challenge on the fourth of July, a little over one month from the point that I wrote the original part of this section, and now almost five months later, I continue to struggle with this task. The challenge was to accept the task that was presented to my daughter. I am not permitted to hurt anything, to speak badly of anyone. I am to look at the positive side of every statement, action, and thought. I must not provide spiritual guidance or recommendations to anyone during the period of this challenge, a period of thirty consecutive days without violation of the rules of the challenge. Over one hundred days after the start of the challenge, I reset almost every two weeks, restarting each time at day zero. I have achieved up to twenty-one days, but am on day two today; I feel good, I feel relaxed. There is nothing that is to take precedence over this challenge, it takes precedence over everything. I must say to you that to accept such a challenge presents such awards that you may not even imagine. To listen and not judge is not very easy to accomplish, but trying to do so is so rewarding. But honestly, it is so difficult to accomplish. With each failure, there is always a lesson learned. I continue, freely, this task.

I chuckle to myself and consider the task. This task is not easy, I am not sure that I completely understand what it is that I must do to succeed. The desire to counsel pushes me, I fail and reset again and again. I look for the reason that I fail and try to explain it. Most times, when thinking about the task, if asked, I will tell you that I cannot do anything but follow the rules. Then, caught off guard, I will respond reflexively to something and have to reset again. Sometimes I think it is my desire not to succeed, that I want to fail. But that is probably not the case. Sometimes I think that I must succeed and will claim a day of success where success did not occur. When I reflect on what happened, then I reset. Of all of this, the thing that seems most probable is the lack of patience. Today, I must think about patience, to look at the message of a lowly and despised insect, the tick. So patient, it can wait up to years for a food source to appear. If I can learn the patience of the tick, perhaps I can make better progress.

Each morning, I take multiple opportunities for simple meditation, after I walk, before I enter the house, before entering the office, just a couple of seconds. There is no requirement that the time be spent at all, let alone for one minute or forty days. There is only the information that if we provide time, each day, to meditate, to absorb God's positive energy, that it will make all the difference. But you ask, "How much time should I spend?" The answer is much simpler than you can imagine, as it is, "I spend enough that I may feel it." What this means is that time does not exist on the spiritual side. So whether I spend five seconds or five days, it does not matter, as they are equal in terms of infinity. Time is not important, the only importance is that I take the time to reflect on the gifts that God has given me, rejoice in my life, and absorb the positive energies from all that God has given.

Let me reflect a moment, to go back and discuss what occurred toward the end of May 2009. I had driven to the lake to check on my boat, and on my return, my son gave me a call. As we talked, I became concerned. His voice sounded strange, he was full of emotion. He began telling me about things that he could see. He cried from the pain. I thought he was intoxicated, I asked if he had been drinking. He stated that he had, that he needed to drink because he had to deliver me a message, and this was the only way he could do it. He told me that I must never reveal to him the contents of that message, I must promise him this. It is for that promise that I will not give you the full details here.

It was the first time that I had encountered him in this state; I was worried and asked where his wife was. He stated that she had gone to see her father but was on the way home. While he talked, I put him on hold and called her to find out how far she was from home. As she was over an hour away, I asked her to call one of his friends who could go to the house immediately to serve as an intervention. You must understand that I was truly worried. I returned to his call, and he was still talking. I asked him a few questions, and he answered each without difficulty, but his voice seemed to drop lower and lower. It seemed that his friend would never get there, but then all of a sudden, my son stopped talking to me and said, "Hey, how good to see you, I wasn't expecting this pleasure."

It was strange from my perspective, as in one second he went from a state that I perceived as completely intoxicated and almost depressive, to completely sober. His friend later told me that he had stood there quietly for a few minutes, observing, and saw the complete change himself and did not know what to make of that transition. After talking for a few minutes, he decided everything was okay and departed. Upon his departure, my son just as suddenly returned to the previous state that had worried me so. It was strange; I had not seen anyone respond to alcohol in this way. Later I would understand this better as the process of moving from a natural state to a spiritual state. I would hear and ultimately see these transitions and learn to both cherish the experience and loathe every second, all at the same time. I would cherish the gift that was given and his willingness to undergo so much to deliver messages to all that would listen. I would loathe it as his father, because of how much I love him and how much I did not wish to see him suffer. Yes, the suffering was extreme and appeared to grow more intense with each session. There was perhaps a relationship to the length of time he was in the state; the longer he was there, the more painful the return to his normal physical state. It was during one of these states in November of 2009 that he drew the picture of the farm shown earlier. This picture he said is a picture of me.

In the introduction, I said that I cannot provide concrete proof of anything that I have told or will tell you; there is no scientific evidence, no pictures other than what I have presented, no recordings, and nothing more that would suggest or provide you specific evidence that could remove any doubt of what I present. I could offer myself as an example if it helps. I could show you the pictures of me with my grandchildren, obese and struggling to walk across the room. I could show you me today, as of this writing, 150 pounds below the point where I began this part of the journey, dropping in weight below 200 pounds for the first time in twenty-seven years. The thing about all of this is that concrete evidence is never provided. You do not see angels strolling about the streets, you do not hear their lectures on the radio or television, you do not hear their recorded voice. The gift to hear is only allowed to a few who seek it, that we may gain encouragement to believe in the power of God's existence and his love. What is left is the choice and ability to deny. If you knew the certainty of their existence, you may become more of a robot or slave to that existence. You would think you have no choice or say in the outcome of your life and thereby not live your life as you choose. To have that choice, you must have the ability to deny truth or to create alternate truths.

Everything that I have presented is real, it is the truth, it is a certainty, but only as far as I am willing to consider it real, to consider it true, and to consider it as certainty. All that I believe as true is true. That same option is given to you; to consider it as truth or not is your choice.

This morning, I took my morning walk with the Bailey. It was a crisp Sunday morning; the sidewalk clear. I did not encounter more than two persons during the walk. My mind wandered from one place to another. At mile two, I thought that I should take the time to hold my hands up at my sides. At mile three, I looked at the light of the morning sunrise. I asked God to help me understand myself, to love myself better, to understand myself that I might understand my role in this world, that I may serve God better. I listened to the birds, at least once thinking that I heard that lonesome northern flicker. I made the final turn toward home, and as I turned up the street toward the house, two Canada geese swooped low down the street, no higher than head level, and as they flew past they called twice, twice directly beside me. Then they swooped up and over the house in front. I watched them fly off and thought about this simple message from God and those who watch over me. So simple these little signs, signs that they are there and that I am not alone. How many times must they prove this to me? How many times have they done so? More times than I can count. It was beautiful, it was comforting, it was glorious. How did I feel? I felt loved!

I have taken time to reflect on what was said and what I understood to be said. I struggle to see and hear them, to hear the tones each morning that are not for me at this point in time. I think of the words in the Bible, the Book of Robes. I try to understand the meaning, I have always been convinced that these books, these chapters, they were written by man for man, as a method of control. If it works, why would I want to change it? Would I create a better plan? It is doubtful that I am that intelligent, but still, it seems that something is missing in what is written.

I captured this statement from his notes:

> *Why that we move with you through time, robes of old to suits of present. That you stay with we at a time, robes of old now robes of present. Thus then, "Why robes?" not heard and now "Why robes?" not understood.*

> *If then, that "is" was we and "that" was you, "is" was said and "that" understood. And now "that" heard and "was" understood, when "is" not heard then, nor understood now.*

I discussed this with Rich, and he explained that it is a metaphor. If I study it carefully, it makes sense. It simply asks why we continue to look into the past to see the angels and the communications from God. They were there then, and they are here now. In the times of the past, they were seen in the same form as those of that time. Today they are seen as each of us are seen, in suits, not robes. That is why today we don't recognize them, as we look for them in robes, not suits.

The next part of what was said is that words are lost in discussion and interpretation, so much so that ultimately what was said then and understood were neither said then nor understood now.
In November 2009, my wife and I traveled to our son's home for a pre-Thanksgiving visit. The preceding days were complex. He was on a path that was getting more and more complex, the pain he experienced was extreme, we talked each evening for hours on the phone, and now we were face to face again. He would later describe the period of this visit as one of the most powerful in terms of the spiritual energies that he had yet encountered. Each day he moved into "in spirit," state one or two, and spoke with me, each night he was "in spirit" and spoke with his wife.

It was during one of these afternoons that we engaged in some very deep conversations, he had been "in spirit" for a couple of hours, and his wife sat down with his mother, there on the patio table, and he asked her to share with me the information that she had received so that I may help her to understand. She was uncomfortable and struggled to share, she was obviously very torn.

She summarized the conversation she had with him that morning. First was a message that she was to pass to me. She had spoken with him this morning, and he gave to her the name, that name that she should give to me. That the true name given to me, given at the time that God reaches down and pulls a thread from his essence and weaves it with his fingers into a soul, at that moment God gives the soul a name, its true name, and that the name that is my true name, given to her to pass to me, is Nathaniel; Nathaniel, my true name.

At this moment in time, we were receiving information of the potential future that could occur, but only if certain choices were made. He was giving lessons on life and understanding when his mother awoke from a nap. He immediately began talking to her. He spoke of protections and shells that build up around the heart. In an effort to give her an example of this type of protection, he grabbed a plastic drinking container from the table, a container half filled with melted ice and soda. He quickly tossed the contents over his shoulder and then went to crush it in his hand. It did not break, and he just smiled again and discussed the point he was trying to make about breaking the shells around the heart. He told her that she would have a long life. She said that she did not want to live that long. He looked at her, took her hand, and said, *"Your line is long, the line of your grandmother, your mother, you, your daughter, and your granddaughter. You will live to see your great-granddaughter, and believe me, when the time comes you will beg God to let you live long enough to see the daughter of your great-granddaughter."*

I asked him about the future, what would occur and when. Like so many times before, he simply answered, *"If you want to know your future, seek a psychic."*

I have chosen to understand this latter statement that a psychic is able to communicate to the spirits and spirit guides, and via the spirit guides gain information of your soul's plan for this time in human form. What I further choose to understand is that he who speaks to me in this way has only one true message to deliver, and that message is that God loves us, each and every one, completely and unconditionally. That love gives us the freedom of choice, and because of that freedom of choice, no path that exists is single or unconditional.

EVOLUTION

Spiritual transition is about evolutionary steps, not revolutionary. I understand within myself that it has taken years for me to get where I am at this point in my life. Each evolutionary step has been necessary to create who I am. My overall personality has been formed by multiple experiences, both positive and negative. For each step forward, I have often taken two steps backward; for each path chosen, multiple branches of that path have been presented; more choices have been presented from which to choose.

In the summer of 1995, my son had a head-on accident that resulted in a closed head injury. The following months, he became increasingly depressed, and in the early part of 1996 he was suffering from bulimia and anorexia. At the same time, in March of 1996, my father entered the hospital, suffering from pulmonary fibrosis; he passed in April. During one of our visits to see my father, on the way home, my son explained to me that he wanted to change places with his grandfather. His grandfather wanted a young body, and he wanted to die. I told my son that this was not acceptable, death was not an option. I don't really know how to explain the ensuing battle to save the life of my son, to bring him back from the depth of darkness where he walked. What I must say is that there is absolutely no way to battle the forces of negative energies except one. If you must do battle, as I so struggled to do, the only way is to love, complete, unfaltering love. I did not understand it then, nor do I completely understand it today. But each and every time my son and I discussed the issues, I could only tell him that I loved him and that I would gladly take his burden if he would only pass it to me. I begged him to trust in God and put his fate in God's hands. He would smile at me and then tell me that he loved me too much to even consider passing to me the burden he carried. *"You have no idea of what you ask, Father, but even if I could, I would never put this on you, I love you too much."*

In late 2001, I was very focused on the completion of my doctorate dissertation. At the same time, I continued my attention on spiritual connections. I read on the Internet about methods for obtaining the identity of your personal spirit guide, and I completed the instructions as described. I woke up one morning with the name of Don on my mind, after asking the night before for his or her name. This was another important evolutionary step that would lead to receiving assistance on solving a complex problem with a programming application. Though the exact details of that solution are too technical to include here, I must tell you that I was perplexed with a programming issue and had purchased a book to help me find the answer. Three times at the electronics store, I had picked up this book and set it aside, but it kept coming back into my hands. I finally conceded and purchased the book. At home, I sat behind my desk and searched the pages for an answer. I read section after section, not finding what I needed. I was tired, frustrated. I walked into the bedroom and lay across the foot of the bed, continuing to search through the book; the doors were open, and a light breeze blew into the room. My head nodded, and then a sudden rush of air flipped the pages. I put my hand onto the book, thinking that I had lost my place where I was reading. I looked down at the book. There at my hand were the instructions that I needed for my program. A simple paragraph that said if you want to do this, you must do that first. So simple, yet this programming routine that I did not know was preventing me from completing my project. I marked the place and then got busy on something else.

Asleep one night, I woke up early in the morning. It was very quiet. I sat up and closed my eyes a moment. There was a strange light approaching me. I opened my eyes, it was dark. I closed my eyes again and once again saw the light. Opening my eyes again, I looked around for anything that could be the source of that light. I did not find anything. I finally just sat back, closed my eyes, and watched the light approach. The light swirled and swirled, getting brighter and more powerful in my mind. My mind was engulfed with the pure whiteness, and then, a thought came into my head: "When are you going to check the box?" First the light, then the thought, then it was all gone. It was a few days later that I completed the programming of the solution shown to me in the book. It was so simple, but sufficient enough for me to complete the work and finalize my research for my degree.

In early 2002, I met with Cyd and asked her about Don. She told me he is my brother from a past life and my current spirit guide for this life. She also told me that in that past life, he had gone fishing with me, his older brother, and had drowned. The thought of this plagued me for many weeks. Each night, I would take the time to talk to him and ask why he had drowned and how had I not saved him. It did not make sense to me that I would survive and he would not. One evening as I sat up in bed, meditating before sleep, a vision flashed within my mind. I saw a tall slender young man, denim pants, no shirt, a funny hat (early settler type), standing there, slightly turned away, but looking back at me. It was quick and clear, then gone. A couple of nights later, I awoke suddenly; someone had run their fingers through my mouth, clearing debris. I coughed and coughed, coughing up water from my lungs, I struggled to breath, I raised up on my hands and knees, gasping for breath. I was drenched, water running from my hair down into my face, my clothes wet, the ground rough on my knees. I gasped and choked, struggling to breathe; then I opened my eyes. I was on my hands and knees, in bed, staring at my pillow. I was completely dry; awake, in bed, alone, on my hands and knees, staring at my pillow.

Evolution is an important part of the process that I am performing. It is not revolution, there are no immediate results. Nothing that I have heard, seen, or felt can of itself be considered any form of miracle, unless you want to consider life a miracle. At first I thought that I could march down the hall and open a door and there it would be, the solution that I seek. Yes, as stated often, I have more than once been the recipient of a solution presented to me, a protection, a push. I did not know that these occurred at the time, and honestly, I only think that they were something more because of what I know is possible now. I have spoke with others about problems that they should try to solve, and in an emotional rush, they have gone out to seek change. That change is only fleeting. It is like stepping outside your home on the East Coast and saying that today you are going to walk to the West Coast, and then, having crossed the street, crying in exaltation on that accomplishment. True, it is good to take that small step, accomplish that small part, but it is only a very small part of the journey. The journey that I see myself on, I believe to be very difficult, full of challenges to overcome. I do this because I want to, today. I don't know what I will want to do tomorrow, but let me tell you that the path to where I was is downhill and already paved. Contrast that to the uphill path that I am on, which is strewn with obstacles and infinite challenges. I ask God for strength to prevail. I am trying not to be overly ambitious. I try to push pride to one side and just live. I call it evolution, because I do not see rapid change. I understand that failures will occur but I try not to create excuses about those failures, just because they are expected.

To listen, think, question, evolve; that is the path that I choose to be on. For each small success I rejoice, for each failure I reflect. That is enough, it does not take more than that. I sit here now, thinking about what I am trying to convey to you in this paragraph. A few days ago, I spoke with him again. He[35] urged me to clear my mind once again. He spoke to me of my questions and offered up answers to any that I may ask. I responded that I was humbled by his presence and that my questions were too trite to seek answers from him. He then reviewed the thousand questions in my mind. What lives have I lived? The answer, many, the most important the first life when Nathaniel was born, and then the current life that I am on. He told me to live this life, worry not about the past. He also talked to her about me. He told her that he had spoke with his brethren about me, they all enjoyed speaking with me. I am thankful, because I look forward to any opportunity to speak with them. Why? Confirmation, perhaps, but I think it is much more than that. It is the support structure that keeps me telling this story of evolution, the strength to continue my fast, to resist temptation. It is about understanding God's love, the message that they carry so well.

---

[35] Rich, "in spirit," state two, the exact transcript is not there so I summarized the conversation with Zophiel, and therefore it is not in the standard italicized format.

So why do I write this book? What qualifies me to present this to you?

This seems like a difficult question, but I have answered it before. This book is about evolution, and the evolution presented here is my own evolution. I cannot keep for myself all that I have discovered, I feel driven to share it with you. As stated in the introduction, there is very little that can be proven, but that is a part of the plan, a part of freedom of choice, the freedom to accept or reject. Because you have gotten to this point, I know that you too are in the pursuit of knowledge. The qualifications I have to write this are simple. They have chosen to share information with me, and because they trust me with this information, then that is enough for me; hopefully it is enough for you. I know as well that the information and gifts from God, as delivered by them, are not restricted to just one or two. The gifts are there for all that ask, and multitudes have been heard and their request answered. They just may not know it. Just recently it was explained to me about prayers that were answered, answered because of love. Just imagine what we could all accomplish if our lives and thoughts were filled with joy and love for ourselves and all others. It's okay, we all have choice, what we do with that choice makes all the difference. "Know that God loves you, so simple, so simple."

A NEW CHALLENGE

It is also important for me to tell you, that as of this moment, I am facing another challenge that is proving to be one of the more complex challenges that I have accepted. For the last few months, I have worked to satisfy the goals of this challenge, that for thirty consecutive days I must see the good in all that is presented before me. In addition, there are other layers of the challenge. One such layer is to withhold my own interpretations of spiritual understanding, until such time that I truly can understand. At first I thought this challenge simple, but over the first three months, I reset an average of every eight days, always starting anew, but with new insight to the complexity of the challenge.

I discussed the last reset with Rich; I had gone twenty-one consecutive days without a miss. Then I faltered and went back to zero. We had just returned from a Thanksgiving holiday with my brother and his family. Mimi and I, Rich and Sumer, and Sissy with her husband and the two grandchildren all loaded up into an eight-passenger vehicle and drove several hours to my brother's home and enjoyed two days of joy with him and his family. Though the vehicle was cramped and the traffic was often heavy, we were able to spend time with family, some of whom we had not seen for many years; that made it all worthwhile. During this time, my brother spoke to me about this challenge and asked if a question was presented to me, and if answering the question would break the rules of my challenge, would I volunteer to break the rules of the challenge, to answer the question, for the greater good of helping the one that asked the question. My response was, no, I could not willingly do that. So when I told my son that, all of a sudden I had failed on my challenge and reset once again, he asked why, what had I done? I told him that I had snapped at his mother. I was searching for clothes in the suitcase and she had said something about what I was doing and I snapped back, criticizing her. He said that it did not make sense. Why would I break the rules of my challenge for something so trite, but not do so for something more important, as asked by my brother? I explained that it had something to do with reflexive behavior. For example, when asked, then it was easy to think about it and consciously choose the correct response. On the other side of emotions, the reflexive side, something happens and without really thinking about it, as a part of years of negative training, a reflexive response jumps out before there is time to stop it. There was a thoughtful moment, and then he explained:

> *What you are experiencing is a lack of patience. Though you have worked on your patience, there is still a beginning and an end to what you are able to endure.*[36]

I had a cold and an acute sinus infection. It was miserable, and I had not gone on a walk for about six days. I missed my walks. In parallel to this, Bailey had pulled a tendon in her hind leg and was limping. She

---

[36]   A lesson and explanation from Rich.

had not been on a walk with me for three weeks. The stress was starting to build in my mind. I began to worry about my tasks, my exercise. Things seemed to get difficult. I stopped for a moment; in the early morning, I let Bailey outside; stepping out with her, I gave her food and then filled the water bowl. After that I looked to the west, toward the mountains, and let the cool air clear my mind. I could hear the morning birds begin to sing, there was a flock of geese flying overhead. I closed my eyes and listened carefully to the morning. I breathed in, breathing in the positive energy, then I exhaled, feeling the negative energy flowing away from me. I smiled and then thanked God for the many gifts he has given me. My walks would resume soon; for that moment, my hound dog and I needed to heal. It was okay, it, the illness, was something else that pulled on the string of patience. If I were to let it, it would pull through my fingers once again. I would rather think of it differently, that this small illness was a gift to help me understand how something so small could make such a difference. I smiled, I think that during my last visit with my grandson, he was not feeling well, and that this illness may have come from him. I would gladly accept this small price to enjoy spending time with his sister and him, it is such a small thing of little importance compared to the benefit received. No, you may be right if you think that it does not have to be a blessing, it may just be life, but I ask you, what better way is there to react? To think of the joy of family and accept the small inconveniences as gifts to help learn patience, or to react with negative emotions? I think I will just consider it a gift and let you make your own conclusion.

Personal Introduction

I think about who I am and how I fit into the universal plans. The concept of a true introduction of one's self, into a public setting, was born into my mind in 1996, on the first day of a class for my master's program. In that particular class, the instructor asked everyone to introduce themselves. As they did so, I began to realize something new: that each person was their job. As they talked, I thought of the cobbler, the baker, the butcher, and how many of our surnames were developed by the profession that we chose or were chosen for us. I understand that in professional meetings we often need to share with others who we are in terms of our qualifications to participate in the discussions of the meeting. But in this class, the importance of establishing a justification for being in the class seemed less important than truly introducing myself, outside of work, but personally. When my turn came, I introduced myself:

> *I am Richard D. Riddle Sr. I was born and raised in the northern Missouri farm land of a poor family. I am a son, a brother, a nephew, an uncle. I am a husband to my wife of twenty-four years. I am a father. I am a student, therefore I seek knowledge through education. I am spiritual (though at that time I did not fully understand spirituality). I am an engineer by profession, though I have had many professions and even now work at multiple endeavors to support my family.*

I then went on to explain my career path and the reason I was attending the class.

Let me now, more than ten years later, having revealed to you the path I have traveled for five decades, formally and completely introduce myself to you:

I am Nathaniel, a name given to me by God when he created my soul, the essence of himself. I have come and gone many times, transitioning from spirit to flesh and flesh to spirit. At this time I am Richard D. Riddle Sr. For this lifetime I was born and raised in the northern Missouri farm land of a poor family. I am a son, a brother, a nephew, and an uncle. I am a husband to my wife of thirty-six years. I am a father, a grandfather, a friend, and a counselor. I have suffered and practiced all of the seven deadly sins. I am a student; therefore I seek knowledge through education at all levels. I am spiritual and seek knowledge, understanding, and courage from God. I am a listener. I listen to the messages given me from the spiritual side, working to separate God's words from all of the other messages to include my own superficial thoughts. I am a seeker; I seek to know the truth at all levels possible. I am covered with many wounds, hidden by multiple layers of wall paper and paint. I am the tenacious soul that works to remove the wall paper and paint, to open the wounds to the light where they may be cleansed and healed. I am frail and human and suffer the temptations of the negative energies. I am the practitioner of positive energy exercises to absorb all that I can from God such that the negative energies are revealed and have no hold upon me. I am the horse, not the bird, I am the author, not the messenger. I am surrounded by God's messengers, my spirit guide, guardian angels, and all that I love and that love me, past and present. I am he who stands before you, humbly telling you the single and most important message that I have ever received and come to accept. That message is the simple truth that God loves you, each and every one, completely and unconditionally!

A SIMPLE PRAYER

Dear heavenly Father, Father of all, whose love is so pure, so simple, so complete. Grant me knowledge, understanding, and sight. That I may know your love, that I might understand the completeness of your love, and that I might see the results of your love. I ask of these things, Father, that I might serve you better.

HIS PRAYER

Heavenly Father, I come to thee in humility, oh Father. I beseech thee, oh heavenly Father. I beg of thee, grant unto me vision, understanding, and courage. Vision, oh heavenly Father, so I may see that which is meant for mine eyes, that I may help others see, see, Father, the love that is you. The love that is you within all. To see that path set before myself, so that with clarity I may follow that path and stay true to thee, oh heavenly Father. Heavenly Father, I beseech of thee understanding. Understanding where vision fails. To understand what it is that I cannot see. To blindly be led to where it is I must go. To understand the love of thee, oh heavenly Father, that is you in all things. And lastly, heavenly Father, I beseech of thee courage. Courage to step forth where vision fails and understanding is unperceived and to continue without doubt. Courage to accept love where it cannot be seen nor understood. But to know that as mortals its existence may guide us to thee.

ABOUT THE AUTHOR

Nathaniel was born again into this life in 1954 as the youngest of four sons in a hard-working family on a farm nestled in northern Missouri. At the age of two, his early life was uprooted as a result of a house fire that consumed all that the family owned, forcing them to move to a farmhouse located within a 200-acre section where one would have to travel fifteen or more miles to arrive at any populated area.

Early life in the country of northern Missouri birthed early personality traits in him as he observed his father work construction and his mother and brothers work to tend the farm and keep the family fed. He often attended family gatherings at the homes of his grandparents, where the majority of his parents' siblings and their children were assembled. His education started at the Meadville Elementary School, Meadville, Missouri, but shortly thereafter moved to the R6 Elementary School in Trenton, Missouri. In 1967, he entered the work force by joining his brothers, moving hay bales for half a cent a bale. With the money earned, he purchased supplies and clothes for school the following year. The year after, he moved to working at a mobile home park, cutting grass and picking up garbage. When he turned sixteen, he took a job as a fry cook for one week before accepting a job at a local grocery store, whereupon he would sack and carry groceries for the next three years as he completed his high school education.

In 1971, he was accepted at the University of Missouri, Rolla for entry in the fall of 1972. He would have been the first in his family to attend a university. However, it was not meant to be, as shortly thereafter his mother and father divorced, and due to differing matters of opinion with his mother, he moved out on his own to care for himself, all before his eighteenth birthday. Not knowing the ins and outs of funding opportunities for college, he did not enter college in the fall of 1972 as planned, but continued to work at the grocery store, until the spring of 1973, when a foolish bet caused him to crash his car. As all hope seemed to disappear from plans that he made for himself, what he could not see was the hidden plan taking shape and beginning to mold the future he was meant to partake in.

"When I let go of what I think I should be, I become what I was meant to be."—Lao Tzu

Later that spring, while working as a cashier, an army recruiter approached him and invited him to an appointment. Soon thereafter, Richard began his dietary struggle, a struggle he would become very familiar with, time and time again over the next many years of his life. Having achieved his weight goal after months of dieting, he was accepted into the US Army basic training program. During Thanksgiving weekend of 1973, the stone slab of his religious fortitude was chipped by a spiritual event that came to initially haunt him. Short on money, he went off post at Fort Gordon, Georgia, to sell a pint of blood at a local blood center. At that time, he had a poor diet and too high of an alcohol intake. This combined with his high anxiety and nervousness led to a speedy blood withdrawal, and shortly thereafter, he fell unconscious. There, during his unconsciousness, as he floated gently downward in the blackness, he came face to face with two overwhelming truths. One, that there were supernatural forces around him, and, two, that there existed a plan.

Although he applied for a duty station in Germany, the so-called fates stepped in again and weaved their fabric of change. It was not Germany that Richard found himself traveling to, but the Republic of Korea. It was there that Richard met his wife and started his own family. His son was born in the early months of 1975 and his daughter in the early months of 1977.

Over a period of twelve years, he would challenge himself countless times in essence to achieve self-driven desires. He always found opportunities to advance his education through local colleges and universities; he passed the College Level Examination Program (CLEP) tests to enhance his career. He applied to and was rejected three times by the Army Selection Board for the Army Officer Candidate School. During this time of strife, stress, and anxiety of failure, another path was being weaved, secretly, in parallel. All his efforts to strive toward excellence, combined with a series of unfortunate and uncontrolled circumstances, led to a ripple in the fabric of his current path, launching him onto his parallel path.

In December of 2002, he was a very large man, weighing over four hundred pounds. He was presented a plan for weight reduction and proceeded to engage in that plan over the next year, which reduced his weight by over one hundred pounds. He held that weight for another six years, and then his weight started rising again. When he had reached a total of 348 pounds, he stood in his shower and called on God to assist him. The next morning, he received a message that made a significant change in his life. There was another message, and he transitioned from a sedentary lifestyle to a life of daily exercise. He takes daily walks by himself, with his hound dog, or with his wife. On January 21, 2011, he crossed below two hundred pounds for the first time in twenty-seven years.

He was obsessed with the concept of wealth and believed that there were many events that could occur that would be life changing. From the period of December 1985 to July 2009, he played the lottery religiously twice a week, every week. Since July 2009, he has not bought another ticket. Something happened, something changed in his life.

He currently resides in Colorado with his wife, where he enjoys morning and evening walks, observing sunrises, sampling scotch and amassing his scotch library, boating and fishing during the summers, spending time with family, engaging in philosophical and religious discussions, conducting positive energy exercises, and managing his office at work (though he may openly deny the success of this last one).

When asked the following questions, he responded as follows:

You walk up to 4.5 miles each day. How did this habit start?

Well, I stepped outside to see a sunrise, but it was blocked by the house across the street. So I jumped in my truck and drove to the end of the subdivision, about a quarter mile away, and there I fell asleep behind the wheel.

Do you still walk to observe sunrises?
Though the morning is my favorite time of day, it is not necessarily the sunrise that I walk to see today, instead I walk to experience the positive energies of all that surrounds me. During these walks, I enjoy listening to the birds, feeling the fresh air, and gazing upon all that the light illuminates. It is a special moment each and every day for my hound dog and myself to experience the sounds, smells, sights, and touch of the many gifts given by God as proof of his unconditional love.

What do you feel gives you the authority to speak on behalf of spiritual evolution?
What is true authority, other than a person who practices something and eventually becomes good at what they practice? Whether I am a master of spirituality or not really depends on who it is YOU are comparing me to. But as far as I am concerned, I compare myself only to the image I see in the mirror. I'm just a dumb ole country boy who has had his share of ups and downs, twists and turns, and witnessed and observed, and continue to observe, a lot of things and events over the course of my life, much of which I couldn't explain up until recently. The story within is mostly a story of MY evolution and how I came to where I am today. It is my hope that someone reading this book will find something of value, or something of strength, or an experience to relate to, that may start a transition of its own, which in turn would lead to another spiritual journey or evolution. Maybe that person's evolutionary tale will lead to the next step in my evolutionary path. Who knows? I tell you what, though, I look forward to the journey and the challenges that await with a renewed vigor, unlike any I have ever had before, inspired by a true love that I hope others come to know.

CPSIA information can be obtained at www.ICGtesting.com
263370BV0C001B/6/P

9 781462 017386